ATHENIAN HOMICIDE LAW

ATHENIAN
HOMICIDE LAW

IN THE AGE OF THE ORATORS

by

DOUGLAS M. MacDOWELL

MANCHESTER
UNIVERSITY PRESS

First published by Manchester University Press 1963
Reprinted 1966
Special edition for Sandpiper Books Ltd, 1999

Published by Manchester University Press
Oxford Road, Manchester M13 9NR
http://www.man.ac.uk/mup

British Library Cataloguing-in-Publication Data
A catalogue record for this book is available from the British Library

05 04 03 02 01 00 99   7 6 5 4 3

ISBN 0 7190 5742 6

Printed in Great Britain by
Bookcraft (Bath) Ltd, Midsomer Norton

I am grateful to Mr. A. R. W. Harrison for reading this book and making a number of helpful comments and criticisms.

D. M. M.

CONTENTS

ABBREVIATIONS

THE ATTIC ORATORS

Ais.	Aiskhines.	Hyp.	Hypereides.
And.	Andokides.	Is.	Isaios.
Ant.	Antiphon.	Isok.	Isokrates.
D.	Demosthenes.	Lyk.	Lykourgos.
Dein.	Deinarkhos.	Lys.	Lysias.

Where the authorship does not affect my argument, I do not distinguish spurious speeches from genuine ones.

OTHER ABBREVIATIONS

Ath.Pol.	the *Athenaion Politeia* attributed to Aristotle.
CP	*Classical Philology.*
Lex.Seg.	*Lexica Segueriana.* References are to page and line of I. Bekker *Anecdota Graeca* volume i (Berlin, 1814).
LSJ	Liddell and Scott *Greek-English Lexicon* (ninth edition, revised by Stuart Jones and McKenzie, Oxford, 1940).
Polyd.	Polydeukes *Onomastikon.*
RE	*Paulys Real-Encyclopädie der classischen Altertumswissenschaft.*
RIDA I, II, III	*Revue Internationale des Droits de l'Antiquité* first series (1948–51), second series (1952–3), third series (1954–).
TAPA	*Transactions of the American Philological Association.*
ZSSR	*Zeitschrift der Savigny-Stiftung für Rechtsgeschichte (Romanistische Abteilung).*

For modern works referred to by the author's name, with or without an abbreviation of the title, see the list on pages ix-x. Other abbreviations are mostly the same as those of LSJ.

LIST OF BOOKS AND ARTICLES

ADKINS, Arthur W. H.: *Merit and Responsibility: a study in Greek values* (Oxford, 1960).

BERGE, H. M. TEN: *Antiphon's Zesde Rede* (Nijmegen, 1948).

BONNER, Robert J.: 'Did Women Testify in Homicide Cases at Athens?' (in *CP* i [1906] 127-32).

— 'Evidence in the Areopagus' (in *CP* vii [1912] 450-6).

BONNER, Robert J., and SMITH, Gertrude: *The Administration of Justice from Homer to Aristotle* (Chicago, 1930-8).

DÜLL, Rudolf: 'Archaische Sachprozesse und Losverfahren' (in *ZSSR* lxi [1941] 1-18).

GERNET, Louis: *Antiphon: Discours* (Paris, 1923).

— 'Sur l'exécution capitale' (in *Revue des Études Grecques* xxxvii [1924] 261-93).

— *Droit et société dans la Grèce ancienne* (Paris, 1955).

GLOTZ, Gustave: *La solidarité de la famille dans le droit criminel en Grèce* (Paris, 1904).

— *Études sociales et juridiques sur l'antiquité grecque* (Paris, 1906).

HARRISON, A. R. W.: 'Drakon's πρῶτος ἄξων' (in *CQ* xi [1961] 3-5).

HEADLAM, J. W.: 'Notes on Early Athenian History I.—The Council: ἐφέται and ναύκραροι' (in *CR* vi [1892] 249-53).

HEWITT, J. W.: 'The Necessity of Ritual Purification after Justifiable Homicide' (in *TAPA* xli [1910] 99-113).

HIGNETT, C.: *A History of the Athenian Constitution* (Oxford, 1952).

JACOBY, Felix: *Atthis: the local chronicles of ancient Athens* (Oxford, 1949).

JONES, J. Walter: *The Law and Legal Theory of the Greeks* (Oxford, 1956).

KAHRSTEDT, Ulrich: *Staatsgebiet und Staatsangehörige in Athen* (Stuttgart, 1934).

KELLS, J. H.: 'Antiphon and Homicide Law' (in *Proceedings of the London Classical Society* i [1947-52] 14-15).

KERAMOPOULLOS, A. D.: Ὁ ἀποτυμπανισμός (Athens, 1923).

LATTE, Kurt: 'Beiträge zum griechischen Strafrecht' (in *Hermes* lxvi [1931] 30-48, 129-58).

— 'Mord' (in *RE* xvi [1933] 278-89).

LIPSIUS, J. H. : *Das attische Recht und Rechtsverfahren* (Leipzig, 1905-15).

MACDOWELL, Douglas M. : *Andokides : On the Mysteries* (Oxford, 1962).

MAIDMENT, K. J. : *Minor Attic Orators* volume i (Cambridge Mass. and London, 1941).

MASCHKE, Richard : *Die Willenslehre im griechischen Recht* (Berlin, 1926).

MEDERLE, Carolus : *De iurisiurandi in lite Attica decem oratorum aetate usu* (Munich, 1902).

MILES, John C. : 'The Court in Phreatto' (in *RIDA* I v [1950] 219-24).

MORROW, Glenn R. : 'The Murder of Slaves in Attic Law' (in *CP* xxxii [1937] 210-27).

MOULINIER, Louis : *Le pur et l'impur dans la pensée des Grecs* (Paris, 1952).

OLIVER, James H. : *The Athenian Expounders of the Sacred and Ancestral Law* (Baltimore, 1950).

OSTWALD, Martin : 'The Athenian Legislation against Tyranny and Subversion' (in *TAPA* lxxxvi [1955] 103-28).

PAOLI, U. E. : *Studi di diritto attico* (Florence, 1930).

— 'Le développement de la "polis" athénienne et ses conséquences dans le droit attique' (in *RIDA* I i [1948] 153-61).

— 'La notion de prorrhésis en droit attique' (in *RIDA* III iii [1956] 135-42).

PHILIPPI, Adolf : *Der Areopag und die Epheten* (Berlin, 1874).

RUSCHENBUSCH, Eberhard : 'Φόνος : zum Recht Drakons und seiner Bedeutung für das Werden des athenischen Staates' (in *Historia* ix [1960] 129-54).

SMITH, Gertrude : 'Dicasts in the Ephetic Courts' (in *CP* xix [1924] 353-8).

THIEL, J. H. : 'De Antiphontis oratione prima' (in *Mnemosyne* II lv [1927] 321-34, lvi [1928] 81-92).

— *Antiphons erste Tetralogie* (Groningen, 1932).

TRESTON, Hubert J. : *Poine : a study in ancient Greek blood-vengeance* (London, 1923).

WEINREICH, Otto : 'Blutgerichte ἐν ὑπαίθρῳ' (in *Hermes* lvi [1921] 326-31).

WIJNBERG, Simon : *Antiphon's Eerste Rede* (Amsterdam, 1938).

WOLFF, H. J. : 'The Origin of Judicial Litigation among the Greeks' (in *Traditio* iv [1946] 31-87).

I

PURPOSES

WHEN a person was killed in Athens, the attitude of the Athenians to the event was a complex one, containing several distinguishable strands. In the first place, the killed person had suffered a wrong, an injury (ἀδικία, ἀδίκημα), and required vengeance or retribution (τιμωρία); and it was the duty of his family to obtain it for him. Sometimes he would give them instructions (ἐπισκήπτειν) to this effect before he died. In Antiphon's speech *Against the Stepmother* the speaker says that such instructions are customarily given by men who are killed, and were given to himself by his own father after he was poisoned.

Ant. 1.29-30. τότε δέ, ἐὰν μὲν δύνωνται καὶ φθάνωσι πρὶν ἀποθανεῖν, καὶ φίλους καὶ ἀναγκαίους τοὺς σφετέρους καλοῦσι καὶ μαρτύρονται, καὶ λέγουσιν αὐτοῖς ὑφ' ὧν ἀπόλλυνται, καὶ ἐπισκήπτουσι τιμωρῆσαι σφίσιν αὐτοῖς ἠδικημένοις· ἃ κἀμοὶ παιδὶ ὄντι ὁ πατήρ, τὴν ἀθλίαν καὶ τελευταίαν νόσον νοσῶν, ἐπέσκηπτεν. ἐὰν δὲ τούτων ἁμαρτάνωσι, γράμματα γράφουσι, καὶ οἰκέτας τοὺς σφετέρους αὐτῶν ἐπικαλοῦνται μάρτυρας, καὶ δηλοῦσιν ὑφ' ὧν ἀπόλλυνται. 'Then, if they have strength and time before dying, they summon their family and relatives, make them witnesses, tell them their killers, and instruct them to avenge the wrong they have received; and these are the instructions which my father gave me when I was a boy, as he was suffering from his tragic final illness. In the absence of relatives, they make statements in writing, and they summon their slaves as witnesses and tell them their killers.'

Lysias's *Against Agoratos* provides a vivid picture of instructions given in expectation of death. The speaker alleges that during the regime of the Thirty in 404/3 Agoratos denounced a number of men to the Thirty, and they were executed. Among them was Dionysodoros. Now the speaker, who is the brother of Dionysodoros's wife, is accusing Agoratos as the man responsible for his death, and in the course of his speech he describes how Dionysodoros, in the last hours before his execution, was visited in prison by his wife, dressed in black, and other members of his family, and gave his final instructions to them.

Lys.13.41-2. ἐναντίον δὲ τῆς ἀδελφῆς τῆς ἐμῆς Διονυσό-
δωρος τά τε οἰκεῖα τὰ αὑτοῦ διέθετο ὅπως αὐτῷ ἐδόκει,
καὶ περὶ ᾿Αγοράτου τουτουὶ ἔλεγεν ὅτι ⟨οἱ⟩ αἴτιος ἦν τοῦ
θανάτου, καὶ ἐπέσκηπτεν ἐμοὶ καὶ Διονυσίῳ τουτῳί, τῷ
ἀδελφῷ τῷ αὑτοῦ, καὶ τοῖς φίλοις πᾶσι τιμωρεῖν ὑπὲρ
αὑτοῦ ᾿Αγόρατον· καὶ τῇ γυναικὶ τῇ αὑτοῦ ἐπέσκηπτε, νομί-
ζων αὐτὴν κυεῖν ἐξ αὑτοῦ, ἐὰν γένηται αὐτῇ παιδίον, φράζειν
τῷ γενομένῳ ὅτι τὸν πατέρα αὐτοῦ ᾿Αγόρατος ἀπέκτεινε,
καὶ κελεύειν τιμωρεῖν ὑπὲρ αὑτοῦ ὡς φονέα ὄντα. 'In my
sister's presence Dionysodoros disposed of his property
as he thought fit ; and he said that Agoratos, the accused,
was responsible for his death, and he instructed me, together with his brother Dionysios here and all his family,
to take vengeance on Agoratos for him ; and, believing
that his wife was pregnant by him, he instructed her that
if she had a child she was to tell him that Agoratos killed
his father, and to command him to take vengeance on
Agoratos for him as his killer.'

But besides obtaining vengeance for the wrong which
the killed person had suffered, it was necessary also to free

the whole state from the pollution incurred by homicide. This is the second strand that can be distinguished in the Athenian attitude to killing. Killers were men with unclean hands (μὴ καθαροὶ τὰς χεῖρας). They had incurred pollution (μίασμα, μιαρία), which affected all with whom they came into contact and the whole of the state in which the crime was committed. To cleanse or purify (καθαίρειν, ἁγνίζειν, ἁγνεύειν) the state was a duty of the family of the killed person. This may be seen clearly in the first of the *Tetralogies* attributed to Antiphon, when opening remarks to the jury are being made by a member of a family prosecuting for homicide.

Ant.2a.3. σαφῶς γὰρ οἴδαμεν ὅτι πάσης τῆς πόλεως μιαινομένης ὑπ' αὐτοῦ, ἕως ἂν διωχθῇ, τό τ' ἀσέβημα ἡμέτερον γίγνεται, τῆς θ' ὑμετέρας ἁμαρτίας ἡ ποινὴ εἰς ἡμᾶς τοὺς μὴ δικαίως διώκοντας ἀναχωρεῖ. ἅπαντος δὲ τοῦ μιάσματος ἀναχωροῦντος εἰς ἡμᾶς . . . 'We well know that, the whole state being polluted by him until he is prosecuted, the religious offence is ours, and for your error the penalty falls on us if we do not prosecute him as we ought. Since the whole pollution falls on us . . .'

All citizens are polluted, but some are more polluted than others. The stain affects the whole state, but it more particularly affects those who associate with the killer, knowingly or even unknowingly.

Ant.5.82. οἶμαι γὰρ ὑμᾶς ἐπίστασθαι ὅτι πολλοὶ ἤδη ἄνθρωποι μὴ καθαροὶ χεῖρας ἢ ἄλλο τι μίασμα ἔχοντες συνεισβάντες εἰς τὸ πλοῖον συναπώλεσαν μετὰ τῆς αὑτῶν ψυχῆς τοὺς ὁσίως διακειμένους τὰ πρὸς τοὺς θεούς, τοῦτο δὲ ἤδη ἑτέρους ἀπολομένους μὲν οὔ, κινδυνεύσαντας δὲ τοὺς ἐσχάτους κινδύνους διὰ τοὺς τοιούτους ἀνθρώπους, τοῦτο δὲ ἱεροῖς παραστάντες πολλοὶ δὴ καταφανεῖς ἐγένοντο οὐχ

ὅσιοι ὄντες, καὶ διακωλύοντες τὰ ἱερὰ μὴ γίγνεσθαι τὰ νομι-
ζόμενα. 'You no doubt know that many men with unclean hands, or having some other pollution, by embarking
on board ship with others have destroyed not only their
own lives but with them men who are in a state of grace;
and also that others, though they have escaped death,
have incurred the greatest dangers because of such men;
and also many, standing beside sacrifices, have been
proved to be impure and to be an obstacle to the performance of the rites.'

It is important to distinguish pollution clearly from the
killed man's need to be avenged. Jones 254 writes of ' this
idea of pollution and family retribution for the shedding of
blood '. But vengeance (τιμωρία) and purification (καθαρ-
μός) are two ideas, not one. Adkins 95 more accurately
writes : ' But whatever may be the relation to " pollution "
of the anger of either the dead man or his relatives, it should
be evident that neither of them *is* " pollution ".' The injury
affects the killed person, and perhaps also the members of
his family ; they are the only persons who require vengeance.
The pollution affects the whole state and all who come into
contact with the killer, though they may never even have
known the killed person and thus are not injured by his
death. The killed person needs vengeance ; the killer and
others associated with him need purification. Nor is there
any necessary causal connexion between the two ideas. It
is not the case, for example, that pollution is the curse of
the killed person which he removes only when he is avenged,
as some have thought (e.g. Maidment 41 : ' He demanded
blood, the blood of his slayer ; and until he had received
satisfaction, his curse lay upon the living ') ; for we hear
of cases in which purification takes place after homicide
although vengeance is obtained only later or not at all (Ant.

6.4: ἄν τις κτείνῃ τινὰ . . . καὶ μὴ ἔστιν ὁ τιμωρήσων, . . . ἀγνεύει τε ἑαυτόν. D.47.70 : ὑπὲρ σεαυτοῦ καὶ τῆς οἰκίας ἀφοσιωσάμενος . . . , ἄλλῃ δὲ εἴ πῃ βούλει τιμωροῦ). Vengeance and purification are two separable aims.

Nor are they the only aims. Prevention is better than cure ; if possible, prospective killers should be deterred from their crime before they commit it, by the knowledge that such crimes are punished. This makes a third object which a prosecutor may urge a jury to accomplish by condemning a killer—an object so important that it gradually edges out vengeance from this speaker's peroration.

> Ant.2c.11. βοηθεῖτε μὲν τῷ ἀποθανόντι, τιμωρεῖσθε δὲ τὸν ἀποκτείναντα, ἀγνεύετε δὲ τὴν πόλιν. τρία γὰρ ἀγαθὰ πράξετε· ἐλάσσους μὲν τοὺς ἐπιβουλεύοντας καταστήσετε, πλείους δὲ τοὺς τὴν εὐσέβειαν ἐπιτηδεύοντας, ἀπολύσεσθε δ᾽ αὐτοὶ τῆς ὑπὲρ τούτου μιαρίας. 'Help the dead man, punish the killer, purify the state. You will thus achieve three good things : you will diminish the number of future criminals, you will increase the number of god-fearing men, and you will free yourselves from the pollution which this man has brought upon you.'

The purpose of this book is to see how this mixture of attitudes was translated into a practical legal system, by giving an account of what is known of Athenian homicide law. The period with which I am mainly concerned is the late fifth and the fourth centuries B.C., the age of the Attic orators. Chronology does not often feature in the discussion. This is partly because changes in Athenian homicide law were seldom made. Antiphon praises it on this account.

> Ant.6.2. καὶ τοὺς μὲν νόμους οἳ κεῖνται περὶ τῶν τοιού-των πάντες ἂν ἐπαινέσειαν κάλλιστα νόμων κεῖσθαι καὶ ὁσιώτατα. ὑπάρχει μὲν γὰρ αὐτοῖς ἀρχαιοτάτοις εἶναι ἐν

τῇ γῇ ταύτῃ, ἔπειτα τοὺς αὐτοὺς αἰεὶ περὶ τῶν αὐτῶν, ὅπερ
μέγιστον σημεῖον νόμων καλῶς κειμένων· ὁ χρόνος γὰρ καὶ
ἡ ἐμπειρία τὰ μὴ καλῶς ἔχοντα διδάσκει τοὺς ἀνθρώπους.
'Everyone would agree that the existing laws on such
matters are the finest and most righteous of laws. They
have the advantage of being the oldest in this country,
and they have always remained unchanged; and that is
the surest evidence of good laws, since time and experience show men what is unsatisfactory.'

Between the time of Antiphon and that of Deinarkhos no
important innovations seem to have been introduced. And
before that period the evidence is too meagre for the chrono-
logical development to be traced. Athenian writers (e.g.
And.1.81-3, D.20.158, 23.51, 47.71, *Ath.Pol.*7.1) commonly
attribute their homicide laws to Drakon, in the late seventh
century, and do not say that any of his laws about homicide
were ever rescinded or changed. The homicide courts of
the Areopagos and the ephetai are assumed to have originated either at that time or earlier. Some scholars have tried
to reconstruct the history of Athenian homicide law in the
seventh and sixth centuries; the most recent attempt is the
article by Ruschenbusch in *Historia* ix. But such recon-
structions rest on insecure foundations. Their authors
commonly begin by taking the texts of laws in force later,
and making deductions from small linguistic details about
the circumstances in which these laws were originally made.
But often the deductions are unsound because such details
are open to many different explanations. For example,
Ruschenbusch bases the very beginning of his argument on
the single word καὶ in *IG* i² 115.11; A. R. W. Harrison (*CQ*
xi [1961] 3-5), by suggesting another explanation of this
word, undermines Ruschenbusch's whole edifice. Secondly,
the reconstructors use statements in authors of the fourth

century and later. Yet these authors probably had little more information than we about the laws of Drakon as distinct from the laws of their own day. The remarks I have just quoted from Ant.6.2 show that Antiphon knew nothing of any developments in homicide law. The date of the establishment of the Areopagos was as doubtful in Plutarch's time as in ours (Plu.*Sol.*19). Hignett (chapter I) provides a good statement of the arguments against the view that much information about the laws of the earlier period survived even in the fifth and fourth centuries. To their deductions from later laws and statements in later authors the reconstructors add some conjectures and speculations about the ways in which they would expect the Athenian legal system to have developed, and sometimes they quote Homer and Hesiod, seemingly unaware that Homer (whether one man or several) and Hesiod were not Athenians and did not write about Athens ; and so they produce their accounts of Drakon's laws. To say that these accounts are completely valueless, or that nothing at all can be known about Athenian homicide law before the fifth century, would perhaps be going too far. But it is in my opinion impossible, with the evidence we at present have, to give a full and reliable account of the system in use before then. Wolff (*Traditio* iv 74) has written : ' The early history of the Areopagus and the various courts of the ephetae is a mystery which will never be fully penetrated unless new sources provide us with clues '. I share his despondency.

So I have nothing to say about Drakon. I describe only the system in use in the age of the orators. I keep as close as I can to the evidence, and quote it fully. There is no point in paraphrasing an Attic orator when he can speak very well for himself, and full quotation will help the reader to check the accuracy of my account.

B

II

THE FAMILY

It was to the killed man himself that vengeance was due, and if before his death he chose to waive his right to it no one else might demand it. A victim might forgive his killer with his dying breath, and then the killer was immune from all prosecution and punishment. Demosthenes states the rule in his speech *Against Pantainetos*.

D.37.59. ἂν ὁ παθὼν αὐτὸς ἀφῇ τοῦ φόνου, πρὶν τελευτῆσαι, τὸν δράσαντα, οὐδενὶ τῶν λοιπῶν συγγενῶν ἔξεστ' ἐπεξιέναι, ἀλλ' οὓς ἐκπίπτειν καὶ φεύγειν, ἂν ἁλίσκωνται, καὶ τεθνάναι προστάττουσιν οἱ νόμοι, τούτους, ἐὰν ἀφεθῶσιν ἅπαξ, ἁπάντων ἐκλύει τῶν δεινῶν τοῦτο τὸ ῥῆμα. 'If the victim himself before he dies absolves the doer from the homicide, no other member of the family may proceed against him, but those for whom, if convicted, the laws ordain expulsion and exile and death, if they are once absolved, are freed from all danger by this utterance.'

But this, we may imagine, seldom happened; indeed no actual instance is recorded. And on all other occasions when a man was killed, it was the duty of his relatives to take appropriate action. To fail to take action was a disgrace—one to which Theokrines is alleged to have submitted himself only because he was bribed.

D.58.28-9. τελευτήσαντος αὐτῷ τοῦ ἀδελφοῦ βιαίῳ θανάτῳ, τοιοῦτος ἐγένετο περὶ αὐτὸν οὗτος, ὥστε ζητήσας τοὺς

8

δράσαντας καὶ πυθόμενος οἵτινες ἦσαν, ἀργύριον λαβὼν
ἀπηλλάγη. . . . ὑπὲρ ὧν δ' ἔπαθεν ἐκεῖνος, μέχρι τούτου
σχετλιάζων περιῄει καὶ φάσκων εἰς "Αρειον πάγον Δημο-
χάρην προσκαλεῖσθαι, ἕως διελύσατο πρὸς τοὺς τὴν αἰτίαν
ἔχοντας. χρηστός γ' ἐστὶ καὶ πιστὸς καὶ κρείττων χρημάτων. οὐδ' ἂν αὐτὸς φήσειεν. ' When his brother died
a violent death, the attitude of Theokrines towards him
was so callous that, after seeking out those responsible
and discovering who they were, he accepted money and
took no further action. . . . For what his brother suffered,
he went around indignantly declaring that he would summon Demokhares on the Areopagos, but he stopped as
soon as he had made a bargain with the men said to be
responsible. He's an honest man, trustworthy, incorrup-
tible ! Why, he wouldn't even say so himself.'

The name for bribes given to avoid prosecution for homicide was ὑποφόνια. (Harp. ὑποφόνια· τὰ ἐπὶ φόνῳ διδόμενα
χρήματα τοῖς οἰκείοις τοῦ φονευθέντος, ἵνα μὴ ἐπεξίωσιν·
Δείναρχος ἐν τῷ κατὰ Καλλισθένους καὶ ἐν τῷ κατὰ Φορ-
μισίου, Θεόφραστος Νόμων ιϛ'. The words ἵνα μὴ ἐπεξίωσιν
show that the purpose was to avoid legal proceedings. So
this passage is not evidence that payment of blood-money
was legal, as some have thought, notably Glotz *La solidarité*
306-21 ; cf. Bonner and Smith ii 196-8.)

Such failure to take action against a killer was not merely
disgraceful. It might also lead to conviction in a law-court.
Diodoros, in the speech *Against Androtion* written for him
by Demosthenes, relates how his uncle was prosecuted by
Androtion for impiety, on the ground that he had associated
with Diodoros on friendly terms although Diodoros was
guilty of parricide.

D.22.2.   αἰτιασάμενος γάρ με, ἃ καὶ λέγειν ἂν ὀκνήσειέ
τις, εἰ μὴ τύχοι προσόμοιος ὢν τούτῳ, τὸν πατέρ' ὡς ἀπ-

ἕκτον' ἐγὼ τὸν ἐμαυτοῦ, καὶ κατασκευάσας ἀσεβείας γραφὴν
οὐκ ἐπ' ἐμέ, ἀλλ' ἐπὶ τὸν θεῖόν μου, γράψας ἀσεβεῖν ἐμοὶ
συνιόντ' εἰς ταὐτὸν ὡς πεποιηκότι ταῦτα, εἰς ἀγῶνα κατέστησεν. ' He made against me accusations which anyone
less brazen than he is would blush even to mention—
that I had killed my own father. He got up a prosecution
for impiety, not against me, but against my uncle, charging
him with impious conduct in that he entered the same
building with me though I was guilty of that act, and he
had him tried.'

There was however no time limit (προθεσμία) within
which the relatives were legally required to take action, or
after which a killer became immune from prosecution. In
Lys.13.83 the speaker says οὐ γὰρ οἶμαι οὐδεμίαν τῶν τοιούτων ἀδικημάτων προθεσμίαν εἶναι, ' There is not, I believe,
any time-limit for taking legal action for crimes of this
kind '. The word οἶμαι appears to imply uncertainty ; but
the statement is shown to be correct by the case of Antiphon's speech *Against the Stepmother*, in which a prosecution
for homicide is brought by the dead man's son, who was
only a boy when his father died (Ant.1.30), so that some years
must have elapsed between the death and the prosecution.
(D.23.80, quoted on page 130, probably refers to the impos-
sibility of prosecuting in the last three months of the year,
for which see pages 34-6 ; thus it is irrelevant to the present
point.) That explains why Androtion's prosecution of
Diodoros's uncle was for associating with Diodoros, and
not merely for failure to prosecute him for homicide.
Although relatives were required by law to prosecute for
homicide, it was normally impracticable to accuse them of
the negative offence of not doing so, because the time-limit
for doing so had never expired, and thus they could always
plead ' But we shall prosecute, all in good time ; we have

not broken the law yet '. There was a time-limit for prosecution for some other offences ; why then was there none
for homicide ? Perhaps because in the case of homicide
the Athenians were particularly anxious that a guilty man
should never escape justice merely because he was not de-
tected early enough.

Granted the obligation of the family to act, two questions
now arise. What relatives were required to take action ?
And what action were they required to take ? These questions sometimes puzzled even the Athenians themselves.
Because the action taken was both religious and legal, two
kinds of authority had to be consulted. The laws of the
state were (at least from the late fifth century onwards) inscribed on stone for all to see. But the rules of religion (or
at any rate some of them) were not published ; knowledge
of them was a prerogative of the exegetai (' expounders '),
and in cases of doubt these officials had to be consulted. In
recent years the exegetai have been discussed in detail by
Jacoby (*Atthis* 8-51) and by Oliver (*The Athenian Expounders
of the Sacred and Ancestral Law*). I shall only give examples
of consultation of them in cases of homicide.

In Plato's *Euthyphron* we hear of a case in which a slave
was killed by a hired labourer on a farm in Naxos. I do
not know whether this case was a real one or merely invented
by Plato, but anyway it illustrates the kind of problem that
was taken to the exegetai.

Pl.*Euthphr*.4c. παροινήσας οὖν καὶ ὀργισθεὶς τῶν οἰκετῶν
τινι τῶν ἡμετέρων ἀποσφάττει αὐτόν. ὁ οὖν πατὴρ συνδή-
σας τοὺς πόδας καὶ τὰς χεῖρας αὐτοῦ, καταβαλὼν εἰς τάφρον
τινά, πέμπει δεῦρο ἄνδρα πευσόμενον τοῦ ἐξηγητοῦ ὅ τι
χρείη ποιεῖν. ' He got drunk and lost his temper with one
of our slaves, and killed him. So my father bound him
hand and foot and threw him into a ditch, and sent a

man to Athens to find out from the exegetes what ought
to be done.'

On this occasion the killer died from starvation and
neglect before the messenger got back to Naxos, and we
are not told what answer the exegetes gave. But a full
account of an answer given by the exegetai appears in the
speech *Against Euergos and Mnesiboulos*. This speech is
number 47 among those attributed to Demosthenes. Now-
adays Demosthenes is generally thought not to have written
it ; but, whoever the author, it is an interesting speech,
both for its lively descriptions of arguments and fights and
for its revealing picture of the extent to which legal decisions
were enforced by private individuals. The original subject
of the dispute was the supply of equipment for a trireme.
The principal disputants were a man named Theophemos
and the speaker of the extant speech, whose name is not
preserved ; I shall call him ' the trierarkhos '. Theophemos
did not produce the equipment which the trierarkhos demanded. The quarrel passed through several stages. At
one point Theophemos won a legal action against the trierarkhos and was awarded damages. The damages were not
paid, and one day, when the trierarkhos was away at Peiraieus,
Theophemos, accompanied by his brother Euergos and
brother-in-law Mnesiboulos, broke into his house and seized
all the property they could lay their hands on. Apart from
some slaves who kept well out of the way, the only people
in the house were the trierarkhos's wife and children and
his old nurse. This woman, originally a slave, had been
freed long before by the trierarkhos's father, but returned to
live in the house after her husband died. At the moment of
Theophemos's irruption lunch was in progress. The old
nurse seized the cup from which she had been drinking and
hid it in her bosom to save it from the marauders, but they

saw it and dragged it from her grasp. She was badly hurt in the struggle, and died a few days later. Theophemos (the trierarkhos claims) was clearly responsible for her death. But the trierarkhos was not a relative of hers. What action ought he then to take? This was the question he took to the exegetai, and I shall quote their reply in full, despite its length, because I shall want to refer from time to time to a number of different points raised in it.

D.47.68–73. ἐπειδὴ τοίνυν ἐτελεύτησεν, ἦλθον ὡς τοὺς ἐξηγητάς, ἵνα εἰδείην ὅ τι με χρὴ ποιεῖν περὶ τούτων, καὶ διηγησάμην αὐτοῖς ἅπαντα τὰ γενόμενα, τήν τε ἄφιξιν τὴν τούτων καὶ τὴν εὔνοιαν τῆς ἀνθρώπου, καὶ ὡς εἶχον αὐτὴν ἐν τῇ οἰκίᾳ, καὶ ὡς διὰ τὸ κυμβίον, οὐκ ἀφιεῖσα, τελευτήσειεν. ἀκούσαντες δέ μου οἱ ἐξηγηταὶ ταῦτα, ἤροντό με πότερον ἐξηγήσωνταί μοι μόνον ἢ καὶ συμβουλεύσωσιν· 69 ἀποκριναμένου δέ μου αὐτοῖς ἀμφότερα, εἶπόν μοι· " Ἡμεῖς τοίνυν σοι τὰ μὲν νόμιμα ἐξηγησόμεθα, τὰ δὲ σύμφορα παραινέσομεν. πρῶτον μὲν ἐπενεγκεῖν δόρυ ἐπὶ τῇ ἐκφορᾷ, καὶ προαγορεύειν ἐπὶ τῷ μνήματι, εἴ τις προσήκων ἐστὶν τῆς ἀνθρώπου, ἔπειτα τὸ μνῆμα φυλάττειν ἐπὶ τρεῖς ἡμέρας. τάδε δὲ συμβουλεύομέν σοι. ἐπειδὴ αὐτὸς μὲν οὐ παρεγένου, ἡ δὲ γυνὴ καὶ τὰ παιδία, ἄλλοι δέ σοι μάρτυρες οὐκ εἰσίν, ὀνομαστὶ μὲν μηδενὶ προαγορεύειν, τοῖς δεδρακόσι δὲ καὶ 70 κτείνασιν. εἶτα πρὸς τὸν βασιλέα μὴ λαγχάνειν· οὐδὲ γὰρ ἐν τῷ νόμῳ ἐστί σοι· οὐ γάρ ἐστιν ἐν γένει σοι ἡ ἄνθρωπος, οὐδὲ θεράπαινα, ἐξ ὧν σὺ λέγεις, οἱ δὲ νόμοι τούτων κελεύουσιν τὴν δίωξιν εἶναι· ὥστ' εἰ διομεῖ ἐπὶ Παλλαδίῳ αὐτὸς καὶ ἡ γυνὴ καὶ τὰ παιδία καὶ καταράσεσθε αὐτοῖς καὶ τῇ οἰκίᾳ, χείρων τε δόξεις πολλοῖς εἶναι, καὶ ἐὰν μὲν ἀποφύγῃ σε, ἐπιωρκηκέναι, ἐὰν δὲ ἕλῃς, φθονήσει. ἀλλ' ὑπὲρ σεαυτοῦ καὶ τῆς οἰκίας ἀφοσιωσάμενος ὡς ῥᾷστα τὴν συμφορὰν 71 φέρειν, ἄλλῃ δὲ εἴ πῃ βούλει, τιμωροῦ." ταῦτα ἀκούσας ἐγὼ τῶν ἐξηγητῶν, καὶ τοὺς νόμους ἐπισκεψάμενος τοὺς τοῦ Δράκοντος ἐκ τῆς στήλης, ἐβουλευόμην μετὰ τῶν φίλων ὅ

τι χρή με ποιεῖν. συμβουλευόντων δέ μοι ταυτά, ἃ μὲν
ὑπὲρ τῆς οἰκίας προσῆκέν μοι πρᾶξαι καὶ ἃ ἐξηγήσαντό μοι
οἱ ἐξηγηταί, ἐποίησα, ἃ δ᾽ ἐκ τῶν νόμων οὐκέτι μοὶ προσῆ-
72 κεν, ἡσυχίαν εἶχον. κελεύει γὰρ ὁ νόμος, ὦ ἄνδρες δικασταί,
τοὺς προσήκοντας ἐπεξιέναι μέχρι ἀνεψιαδῶν (καὶ ἐν τῷ
ὅρκῳ διορίζεται ὅ τι προσήκων ἐστίν), κἂν οἰκέτης ᾖ, τούτων τὰς ἐπισκήψεις εἶναι. ἐμοὶ δὲ οὔτε γένει προσῆκεν ἡ
ἄνθρωπος οὐδέν, εἰ μὴ ὅσον τιτθὴ γενομένη, οὐδ᾽ αὖ θερά-
παινά γε· ἀφεῖτο γὰρ ὑπὸ τοῦ πατρὸς τοῦ ἐμοῦ ἐλευθέρα
73 καὶ χωρὶς ᾤκει καὶ ἄνδρα ἔσχεν. ψεύσασθαι δὲ πρὸς ὑμᾶς
καὶ διομόσασθαι αὐτὸς καὶ τὸν υἱὸν καὶ τὴν γυναῖκα οὐκ ἂν
ἐτόλμησα, οὐδ᾽ ἂν εἰ εὖ ᾔδειν ὅτι αἱρήσοιμι αὐτούς· οὐ γὰρ
οὕτως τούτους μισῶ, ὡς ἐμαυτὸν φιλῶ. ' When she died,
I went to the exegetai to find out what I ought to do
about it. I told them the whole story : the arrival of
these men, the woman's loyalty, how I kept her in my
house, and how she died because of the cup, through not
letting go. After hearing my account the exegetai asked
me whether I wanted them merely to expound or to give
69 advice as well. Both, I answered. " Very well," they
said to me, " we will expound to you what is lawful, and
advise what is expedient. First, you are to bring a spear
to the funeral, and proclaim at the tomb for any relative
of the woman, and then watch at the tomb for three days.
And we give you the following advice. Since you were
not present yourself, but only your wife and children,
and there are no others to act as witnesses for you, do not
make proclamation to anyone by name, but only to ' the
doers and killers '. Next, do not bring a case before the
70 basileus ; it is not legally your concern, since, from what
you say, the woman is not a relative or slave of yours, and
it is for these that the laws order prosecution to be undertaken ; so that if you yourself and your wife and children
take the oath at the Palladion and invoke destruction on

yourselves and your house, many will think you ignoble,
and if he is acquitted you will be thought to have committed perjury, and if he is convicted you will be unpopular. You should just do what religion requires for
yourself and your household, and endure your misfortune
as calmly as you can ; get your revenge in some other
71 way, if you wish." After the exegetai had told me this,
and I had inspected the laws of Drakon on the stone, I
discussed with my family what I should do. When they
gave me the same advice, I did what it was proper for
me to do for my household and what the exegetai had
expounded to me, but I did not go beyond what was
72 proper for me according to the laws. For the law, gentlemen of the jury, orders the relatives to take proceedings,
as far as sons of cousins (it also defines in the oath what
constitutes a " relative ") ; and if he is a slave, these are
to make the denunciations. But the woman was not
related to me at all, except that she had been my nurse ;
nor was she my slave, for she had been freed by my
73 father, and lived separately and had a husband. And I
should not have dared to lie to you and take the oath for
myself, my son, and my wife, not even if I were sure of
getting these men convicted ; for I do not hate them as
much as I love myself.'

For the student of Athenian homicide law this whole
passage repays very careful study. It illuminates several
stages of legal procedure, and it also makes an interesting
distinction between religious and legal requirements. I
shall recur to it several times in later chapters. But at the
moment I am concerned with the exegetai. The problem
which the trierarkhos takes to them, like the one sent to
them by Euthyphron's father, concerns action ($\H{o} \ \tau\iota \ \mu\epsilon \ \chi\rho\grave{\eta}$
$\pi o\iota\epsilon\hat{\iota}\nu$, ' what I ought to *do* ' ; cf. Pl.*Euthphr*.4c $\H{o} \ \tau\iota \ \chi\rho\epsilon\acute{\iota}\eta$
$\pi o\iota\epsilon\hat{\iota}\nu$), and their reply is equally practical. They do two

things : they expound, and they advise. Where they expound, they are the authorities, and must be obeyed ; this is in the religious ceremony of the funeral, with the bringing of the spear (which is a symbol that the deceased died a violent death; cf. Harp. ἐπενεγκεῖν δόρυ, Polyd.8.65, *Dikon Onomata* in *Lex.Seg.*188.14-15, *Lexeis Rhetorikai* in *Lex.Seg.* 237.30-2) and the proclamation and watching at the tomb. Advice, on the other hand, they give hesitantly, asking the recipient's permission before they give it. This concerns the proceedings in a law-court (the advice section of their speech is the part introduced by τάδε), and here they have no authority, and their recommendation is unofficial. Consequently the trierarkhos does not accept it without question, but consults the other members of his family. (οἰκία means persons living in his own house, while φίλοι is a wider term, including such relatives as brothers and cousins. All of these might be involved in a prosecution for homicide, as we shall see shortly. For this sense of φίλοι, compare And.1.118, Lys.13.41, 32.11-12.) On a strict definition, legal procedure is outside the province of the exegetai, and for further enlightenment on it we, like the trierarkhos, must turn our attention to ' the laws of Drakon '.

According to the law which the trierarkhos found on the stone, the obligation to prosecute fell on relatives ' as far as sons of cousins '. (In Polyd.8.118 we find : φόνου δὲ ἐξῆν ἐπεξιέναι μέχρις ἀνεψιῶν, καὶ ἐν τῷ ὅρκῳ ἐπερωτᾶν τίς προσήκων ἐστὶ τῷ τεθνεῶτι· κἂν οἰκέτης ᾖ, ἐπισκήπτειν συγκεχώρηται. The language of this sentence is so like that of the trierarkhos's sentence that it is certainly based on it, as was concluded after a detailed discussion by Philippi 79-84. It therefore has no independent authority ; and consequently the minor differences are of no importance, and time need not be wasted in wondering, for example, what ἐπερωτᾶν can possibly mean in the context of an oath.) The preserved law about unintentional homicide also contains a section specifying the relatives who are to take part in the prosecution.

IG i² 115.20-3 (restored from D.43.57).

[προειπεῖν δὲ τôι] κ-
τέ[ναντι ἐν ἀ]γορ[ᾶι ἐντ]ὸ[s ἀνεφσιότετος καὶ ἀνεφσιὸ· συν-
διόκε]ν
δὲ [καὶ ἀνε]φσ[ιὸs καὶ ἀνεφσιôν παῖδας καὶ γαμβρὸς καὶ πεν-
θερὸ]s [κ]-
αὶ φ[ρά]τ[ε]ρ[αs.]

' Relatives within the degree of cousin's son and cousin are to make proclamation to the killer in the agora ; the prosecution is to be shared by cousins, sons of cousins, sons-in-law, fathers-in-law, and members of the phratry.'

The verbs of the law are jussive infinitives : ' Relatives are to make proclamation . . . '. The form of expression leaves one point obscure : could these actions be undertaken by persons who were not relatives within the specified degrees ? Does ' Relatives are to . . . ' necessarily imply ' All other persons are not to . . . ' ? Modern scholars have generally taken for granted that it does. Their assumption is based not only on the text of the law but also on the belief that homicide cases were never *graphai* but always *dikai*. In *graphai* prosecution was open to ' anyone who wishes ' (ὁ βουλόμενος), but not, it is thought, in *dikai*. However, cases of homicide, though called δίκαι φόνου, were not quite like other *dikai*. They had special courts and special rules. In other *dikai* the accuser was normally the person who had suffered the offence, but in a case of homicide the accuser could never be the person who had been killed. So an analogy with other *dikai* is not a reliable guide to the procedure in homicide cases. We must go not by the laws about other *dikai*, but by the law about prosecution for homicide. And this law is not explicit. It orders relatives to take action ; and of course if relatives took action in a particular case there would be no reason for anyone else to take it, and no problem would arise. But what was to happen if there were no relatives ? Could other persons take action or not ? The law simply does not say. This is the problem that faced the trierarkhos.

The law does make clear that there were two actions to be undertaken by members of the dead man's family : the proclamation and the prosecution. The proclamation was to be undertaken by fairly close relatives, within certain degrees. ' Within ' (ἐντός) means ' as far as and including '. ' Cousin ' (ἀνεψιός) means ' first cousin '. ἀνεψιότης is the relationship of the son of a first cousin, or in other words first cousin once removed (D.43.62-3). (LSJ's definitions of these three words are defective.) Relatives who counted as being within this degree were father, and any other surviving ancestors in the direct male line, sons, and any other male descendants, brothers, uncles, first cousins, and sons of first cousins. (Of course only adult males could take legal action in Athens.) We hear of individual homicide cases in which the initiative was taken by the dead person's son (Ant.1), his father (Ant.3, an imaginary case), and his brother (Ant.6). Relatives outside this category had to share in the prosecution ; this presumably means that they were not required to initiate any legal action, but only to give any support for which the closer relatives asked them. The wider category of relatives included all members of the dead person's phratry (' brotherhood ' or ' clan '), whose relationship to him might be very remote indeed.

If the person killed was not an Athenian citizen but only a metic (μέτοικος) or a foreigner (ξένος), the procedure was still similar ; only his relatives were required to take action. This is clear from the case of the trierarkhos and his old nurse. The nurse was free, but not a citizen. Though the trierarkhos does not actually say so, it is likely that she was a metic and he was her patron (προστάτης). Yet he was not obliged to proceed against her killers, because he was not her relative. At the same time, that did not absolutely prevent him from prosecuting her killers. This is shown by the fact that the exegetai gave him other reasons for not prosecuting. First, no one witnessed the killers' action except the trierarkhos's own wife and children. This meant that if he did prosecute he might find difficulty in proving his case ; and if as a result he lost the case, everyone would conclude that he committed perjury when he swore at the beginning of the trial that Theophemos and Euergos were the killers. Again, even if he won the case, he would be unpopular, presumably because people would think that his motive for bringing the case was malice towards Theophemos. And it would be beneath his dignity (χείρων δόξεις εἶναι) to take as much trouble to obtain vengeance for an old freedwoman as he would for a member of his own family. All this implies that he was not forbidden by law to prosecute ; the exegetai merely advised him not to do so. (This is why in D.47.70 the correct accentuation is οὐδὲ γὰρ ἐν τῷ νόμῳ ἐστί σοι, ' it is not legally your concern ', rather than . . . ἔστι σοι, ' you are not legally permitted to do so '.) The law said that the relatives were to prosecute ; it did not order others to prosecute, but neither did it order them not to.

The only other individual case of the killing of a metic of which details are preserved is that of Lysias 12 (*Against Eratosthenes*). But it is exceptional. This speech was probably not delivered at a trial for homicide but on the occasion

of Eratosthenes's *euthynai*. Consequently nothing can be
deduced from it about the procedure in homicide prosecutions.

If the person killed was a slave, the situation was rather
different. Slaves were of several kinds. The most important
distinction was between slaves belonging to the state or to a
temple (δοῦλοι δημόσιοι or ἱερόδουλοι) and slaves belonging
to the household of an individual master (οἰκέται). About
the first kind there is no evidence relating to homicide ; it
is possible that their position was similar to that of metics.
But about household slaves we have some information.
From the answer given by the exegetai to the trierarkhos
(D.47.70) it appears that if the nurse had been his slave it
would have been right and proper for him to take legal
action against her killers, and he would not have waited for
any initial move by her relatives. An interesting distinction
is made in the law which the trierarkhos found on the stone
(D.47.72). If a free person is killed, his relatives are to proceed against the killer (ἐπεξιέναι), but if a household slave
is killed, the only duty of his relatives is ἐπισκήψεις. Philippi
81-2 proposed to emend τούτων to τῶν δεσποτῶν, in order
to obtain the meaning ' the masters are to prosecute '. But
the term ἐπίσκηψις is not used elsewhere of prosecution for
homicide, and it is not likely that ἐπισκήψεις εἶναι would
have been written here instead of ἐπεξιέναι, which was used
in the earlier clause, unless some distinction of meaning was
intended. ἐπισκήπτειν is the verb used of a dying man who
urges his family to obtain vengeance for him (e.g. Ant.1.29-
30, Lys. 13.41-2, quoted on pages 1-2). So, I suggest, the
duty of the relatives of a killed slave was simply to urge his
master to obtain vengeance for him by taking legal action
against the killer. But the master might take legal action
anyway, even if he received no such urging. Probable in-

stances are recorded in Isok.18.52-4, D.59.9-10. The trials on these two occasions pose another problem, which is discussed in chapter V, but in each case there is no reason to doubt that the prosecutor of the alleged killer of a slave was the slave's master.

Plato makes Kallikles deplore the life of a slave as being worse than death, and one of the reasons given is that when wronged a slave can help neither himself nor a relative (Pl.*Grg.*483b : ἀδικούμενος καὶ προπηλακιζόμενος μὴ οἷός τέ ἐστιν αὐτὸς αὑτῷ βοηθεῖν μηδὲ ἄλλῳ οὗ ἂν κήδηται). He had to rely on his master to obtain vengeance for him. But perhaps the worst plight was that of a slave killed by his own master, for he might have no one at all to obtain vengeance for him. A slave would be unlikely to have any relatives in Athens who had the right to take legal action, and if his own master killed him there would probably be no one else willing to take the trouble of obtaining vengeance for him and to incur odium by prosecuting an Athenian citizen for the benefit of a mere slave who was not his own. In Ant.6.4 it is said that if a man kills one of the persons who belong to himself and have no one to obtain vengeance for them (ἄν τις κτείνῃ τινὰ ὧν αὐτὸς κρατεῖ καὶ μὴ ἔστιν ὁ τιμωρήσων), it is nevertheless customary for him to take religious action to purify himself. This shows that a master who killed his own slave would often go unprosecuted. But it does not prove that he could not be prosecuted. The speaker in Ant.5.47 maintains that the relatives of Herodes acted illegally in putting to death a slave whom they had bought. Admittedly he has an ulterior motive for attacking their action ; still, there is no proof that he is not right, and they may well have been liable to a prosecution for homicide, if any Athenian citizen cared to bring one. There is no evidence that a prosecution for homicide of a slave could not legally be brought by persons other than the slave's master or relatives.

So much for the problem of what persons were obliged by law to take action. The next question is : what action did they take ? Some parts of the procedure for initiating a prosecution for homicide are revealed by a passage of Antiphon 6 (*On the Chorister*). The person who has died is a boy named Diodotos, a member of a chorus rehearsing for the festival of the Thargelia. The speaker, who is accused of causing his death by poison, was the manager of the chorus (χορηγός). His name is not recorded ; I shall call him ' the khoregos '. The leading prosecutor is Philokrates, Diodotos's brother. In his defence the khoregos impugns the sincerity of Philokrates. At the time of Diodotos's death, he says, he himself had begun taking steps to prosecute Aristion, Philinos, and others for embezzlement, and these men bribed Philokrates to bring a homicide charge against him in the hope of preventing him from going on with the embezzlement case. Philokrates and the other members of Diodotos's family are alleged to have proceeded with the homicide charge or abandoned it whenever they received or did not receive bribes from Aristion, Philinos, and their associates.

The khoregos's picture of his opponents' actions and motives probably ought to be regarded with suspicion. But its frame of legal procedure is likely to be sound. A speech to an Athenian jury might not be true, but it would have to be plausible. So, for example, when the khoregos claims that Philokrates was insincere when he made his proclamation against the alleged killer, that does not prove that Philokrates really was insincere, but it does prove that proclamations were made against alleged killers. The procedure began at the point at which Aristion, Philinos, and their associates are said to have bribed Philokrates and his family to prosecute the khoregos.

Ant.6.35-6. πείσαντες δὲ τούτους ἀπογράφεσθαι καὶ προαγορεύειν ἐμοὶ εἴργεσθαι τῶν νομίμων, ἡγήσαντο ταύτην σφίσιν ἔσεσθαι σωτηρίαν καὶ ἀπαλλαγὴν τῶν πραγμάτων ἁπάντων. ὁ γὰρ νόμος οὕτως ἔχει, ἐπειδάν τις ἀπογραφῇ φόνου δίκην, εἴργεσθαι τῶν νομίμων· καὶ οὔτ' ἂν ἐγὼ οἷός τ' ἢ ἐπεξελθεῖν εἰργόμενος τῶν νομίμων . . . 'When they persuaded these men to charge me and make a proclamation to me to keep away from the legal things, they thought that this would be their salvation and escape from all their troubles. For the law runs thus : " Whenever anyone is charged with homicide, he is to keep away from the legal things ". I should not be able to proceed against them while keeping away from the legal things . . .'

The account shows that the two actions which initiated a homicide prosecution were making a charge (ἀπογράφεσθαι) and making a proclamation (προαγορεύειν). This emerges also from the reply of the exegetai to the trierarkhos (D.47.69, quoted on page 13). In that passage two proclamations are mentioned. The first was to be made at the time of the funeral ; this was a religious matter, and formed no part of the legal proceedings. In the second part of their reply, when they cease expounding and begin giving advice about the possibility of taking legal action, the exegetai mention a proclamation to ' the doers and killers ' and the bringing of a charge to the basileus, who was the official in charge of homicide trials.

The legal proclamation by the relatives in the agora we have already met in *IG* i² 115.20-1, and the relatives responsible for it have been discussed. In *Ath.Pol.*57.2 we are told that the basileus made a proclamation (in an account of the functions of the basileus : ὁ προαγορεύων εἴργεσθαι τῶν

c

νομίμων οὗτός ἐστιν). A similar statement appears in *Lexeis Rhetorikai* (*Lex.Seg.*310.6-8 : ὁ βασιλεὺς . . . προαγορεύει τὸν ἀνδροφόνον εἴργεσθαι τῶν νόμων [which probably should be emended to νομίμων]), and in Polyd.8.90 too the basileus is said to proclaim to those who are accused that they are to stay away from ' mysteries and the other legal things ' (προαγορεύει δὲ τοῖς ἐν αἰτίᾳ ἀπέχεσθαι μυστηρίων καὶ τῶν ἄλλων νομίμων). So altogether three proclamations were made :

A : the proclamation at the tomb of the killed person, on the occasion of the funeral. This is the first of the two proclamations mentioned in D.47.69. It was a religious ceremony, with no legal significance. The only thing we know about its content is that the trierarkhos was to appeal for relatives of the nurse to come forward. This would be superfluous on occasions when the relatives of a killed person themselves conducted the funeral, and it may be that on those occasions no such proclamation was made.

B : the proclamation in the agora. This is the one mentioned in *IG* i² 115.20-1 and Ant.6.35, and the second one in D.47.69. It was distinguished from *A* in several ways. First, it was made in a different place. (According to *IG* i² 115.20-1 it was made in the agora. In D.59.9 we read προεῖπεν αὐτῷ ἐπὶ Παλλαδίῳ φόνου, but possibly this means only that the trial was to be held at the Palladion, not that the proclamation was made there.) Secondly, it was a legal action, not a religious ceremony. Thirdly, instead of being addressed to the relatives of the killed person, it was addressed to the killer ; it commanded him ' to keep away from the legal things '. The persons whose duty it was to make this proclamation were the relatives of the killed person. They would normally name the killer whom they addressed, so that the proclamation was practically equivalent to a public announcement of the prosecution which would follow. When the trierarkhos made this proclamation for his old nurse, it was exceptional in two ways : it was made voluntarily by a non-relative, because no relative was available ; and (if he followed the advice of the exegetai) it was not addressed to any person by name, but only to ' the doers and killers ', because no prosecution was intended.

C : the proclamation by the basileus (*Ath.Pol.*57.2, Polyd. 8.90, *Lexeis Rhetorikai* in *Lex.Seg.*310.6-8). This must have been made after the relatives submitted their charge to the basileus, whereas B might be made before the charge was submitted (for the trierarkhos was able to make B without submitting a charge to the basileus at all). Like B, it ordered the killer ' to keep away from the legal things '. There is no information about the place where it was made.

What were ' the legal things ' from which, in both B and C, the killer was ordered to keep away ? Polyd.8.90 specifies ' mysteries '. Demosthenes gives a longer list in a sentence of his speech *Against Leptines* in which he speaks of Drakon and his laws about homicide.

> D.20.158. γράφων χέρνιβος εἴργεσθαι τὸν ἀνδροφόνον, σπονδῶν, κρατήρων, ἱερῶν, ἀγορᾶς, πάντα τἄλλα διελθὼν οἷς μάλιστ' ἄν τινας ᾤετ' ἐπισχεῖν τοῦ τοιοῦτόν τι ποιεῖν.
> ' Ordaining that the killer should keep away from holy water, libations, bowls of wine, holy places, and the agora, and listing everything else which he thought would best restrain people from that kind of offence.'

The proclamations are not explicitly mentioned in this passage, but it can be assumed that the things which an accused killer was ordered to avoid in the proclamations were the same as the things which a killer was ordered to avoid in the laws. Again, the khoregos says that he could not proceed with a prosecution for embezzlement ' while keeping away from the legal things ' (Ant.6.36) ; so it is clear that courts of law (except of course the one in which he himself was tried) were among the places which the accused killer had to avoid, and that one of the effects of the proclamations was to prevent a person charged with homicide from taking any other kind of legal action until his own trial had been held.

Until the proclamation by the basileus had been made, the man accused of killing suffered no legal disability. This is shown by Ant.6.38, where the khoregos relates that because the basileus refused to accept the charge against him he was able to continue his prosecution for embezzlement. This refutes the view expressed by Paoli (*RIDA* III iii 135-142), that a killer suffered legal disfranchisement (ἀτιμία) from the moment when he committed homicide, whether any proclamation had been made against him or not. But once the proclamation had been made, if the accused man went to any of the forbidden places, he was liable to be arrested, imprisoned, and prosecuted by *apagoge*, which was a normal procedure against a person found exercising rights to which he was not entitled. The law is quoted in the speech *Against Timokrates*.

D.24.105. ἐὰν δέ τις ἀπαχθῇ, τῶν γονέων κακώσεως ἑαλωκὼς ἢ ἀστρατείας ἢ προειρημένον αὐτῷ τῶν νομίμων [Salmasius : νόμων codd.] εἴργεσθαι εἰσιὼν ὅποι μὴ χρή, δησάντων αὐτὸν οἱ ἔνδεκα καὶ εἰσαγόντων εἰς τὴν ἡλιαίαν, κατηγορείτω δὲ ὁ βουλόμενος οἷς ἔξεστιν. ἐὰν δ' ἁλῷ, τιμάτω ἡ ἡλιαία ὅ τι χρὴ παθεῖν αὐτὸν ἢ ἀποτεῖσαι. ἐὰν δ' ἀργυρίου τιμηθῇ, δεδέσθω τέως ἂν ἐκτείσῃ. 'If anyone is arrested, being caught maltreating his parents, or evading military service, or going where he should not after a proclamation has been made to him to keep away from the legal things, the Eleven shall imprison him and bring him before the people's court, and anyone who wishes, of those who have the right, shall be the prosecutor. If he is convicted, the people's court shall fix the penalty which he should suffer or pay. If a fine is fixed, he shall be imprisoned until he pays it.'

There is no information about details of the procedure followed in making the charge (ἀπογράφεσθαι). The person who received the charge was the basileus (Ant.6.42), and it was he who was responsible for making arrangements for a trial ; I examine his functions in chapter III. The remaining duty of the family of the killed man was to present the case for the prosecution at the trial. As we have already seen from *IG* i² 115. 21-3, all members of the family and phratry were required by law to assist in the prosecution. But this can hardly mean that they were all required to speak ; it probably means simply that all were responsible for seeing that the prosecution was made. No doubt a single member of the family, commonly the closest relative of the killed man, would make the main speech or speeches for the prosecution, though one or two other members might make supporting speeches.

A special difficulty faced the family when the killing had taken place outside Attica. If, for instance, an Athenian was killed in Thebes by a Theban, the killer would not be likely to come of his own accord to Athens to be tried. In such a case the relatives of the killed man were permitted by Athenian law to seize any three Thebans (or persons of whatever state it was in which the killer was residing) and hold them as hostages until the killer was extradited to Athens. Such seizure was called *androlepsia*, and the right to make it *androlepsion*. (On the distinction between the two words, see Lipsius 267 note 10.) Demosthenes quotes the law in the speech *Against Aristokrates*.

D.23.82. ἐάν τις βιαίῳ θανάτῳ ἀποθάνῃ, ὑπὲρ τούτου τοῖς προσήκουσιν εἶναι τὰς ἀνδροληψίας, ἕως ἂν ἢ δίκας τοῦ φόνου ὑπόσχωσιν ἢ τοὺς ἀποκτείναντας ἐκδῶσι. τὸ δὲ ἀνδρολήψιον εἶναι μέχρι τριῶν, πλέον δὲ μή. (I emend τὴν δὲ ἀνδροληψίαν in the second sentence to τὸ δὲ ἀνδρολήψιον on the evidence of D.23.83-4.) ' If someone dies a violent death, on his behalf his relatives are to make *androlepsiai*, until they either undergo trials for homicide or deliver up the killers. The *androlepsion* is to be up to three persons, not more.'

The law is obscurely worded, but later compilers give more information which clarifies some features.

Polyd.8.50-1. ἀνδρολήψιον δέ· ὅταν τις τοὺς ἀνδροφόνους καταφυγόντας ὥς τινας ἀπαιτῶν μὴ λαμβάνῃ, ἔξεστιν ἐκ τῶν οὐκ ἐκδιδόντων ἄχρι τριῶν ἀπαγαγεῖν. ὁ δὲ ἀδίκως ἀνδρολήψιᾳ κεχρημένος οὐκ ἀνεύθυνος ἦν. '*Androlepsion* : when the killers have taken refuge with some people, and one demands them and does not get them, one is permitted to arrest up to three persons from those who will not deliver up the killers. One who employed *androlepsia* unjustly was not unaccountable.'

Lexeis Rhetorikai in *Lex.Seg.*213.30-214.2. ἀνδρολήψιον καὶ ἀνδροληψία· ἀνδρολήψιόν ἐστι τὸ φόνου πραχθέντος ἔν τινι πόλει, καὶ τοῦ φονέως μὴ ἐκδιδομένου ὑπὸ τῶν πολιτῶν, τρεῖς ἀντ' αὐτοῦ τῶν ἐκείνου πολιτῶν ἄγειν εἰς δικαστήριον, δίκην ὑφέξοντας τοῦ φόνου, καὶ τοῦτο ἀνδρολήψιον καλεῖται. '*Androlepsion* and *androlepsia* : *androlepsion* is, homicide having been committed in some city and the killer not being delivered up by the citizens, to bring to a law-court three of his fellow-citizens instead of him, to undergo trial for homicide ; this is called *androlepsion*.'

There still remain a few problems raised by this law. Were the seizures made in Thebes (to continue my example)

or in Athens ? We are not told ; but one would imagine that
it would be easiest for the family to seize any three Thebans
who happened to be visiting Athens. More difficult : if a
Theban, having killed an Athenian in Thebes, then fled to
(say) Megara, did the family seize three Thebans or three
Megarians ? Demosthenes, contrasting the law with the
proposal made by Aristokrates, insists that the law allowed
seizure only of the citizens of the state in which the homicide
was committed, and says that to demand the extradition of a
refugee is contrary to the universal law that fugitives are to
be received (D.23.85 : τὸν κοινὸν ἀπάντων ἀνθρώπων νόμον,
ὃς κεῖται τὸν φεύγοντα δέχεσθαι). This should mean that the
family might seize three Thebans but not three Megarians ;
and Lipsius 268 note 11 accepts this conclusion, which is
supported by the account in *Lexeis Rhetorikai*. But the
account of Polydeukes clearly points the opposite way ; and
(what is more significant) Demosthenes himself later in the
speech contradicts what he said earlier (contrast D.23.84 παρ'
οἷς ἂν τὸ πάθος γένηται with D.23.218 παρ' οἷς ἂν ὁ δράσας
ᾖ), which leads one to suspect that his interpretation of this
point of the law may be misleading, either deliberately
(because he wishes to make the proposal of Aristokrates to
penalize those who harbour a killer of Kharidemos sound as
different as possible from the existing law) or else accidentally. It is hard to see how the Thebans could be expected
to deliver up a man who was in Megara. So the more
probable (though not quite certain) conclusion is that the
persons who could be seized were citizens of the state in
which the killer now was.

The fellow-citizens of the hostages as a rule would doubtless take swift action to extradite the killer and get them re-
leased. Lipsius 267 says that alternatively they might try
the killer themselves. But this must be wrong ; δίκας ὑπό-

σχωσιν cannot mean ' hold trials '. The normal meaning of δίκην ὑπέχειν is ' undergo justice ', the subject being a person who is tried or punished or both. Miles (*RIDA* I v 222-4) takes the phrase here to mean ' pay compensation '. It is true that in Isok.20.17 this expression is used of a financial penalty ; but since there is no adequate evidence that financial compensation for homicide was ever acceptable in Athenian law (cf. page 9), it is most unlikely that the expression has that sense here. Demosthenes thought that it meant that there was a trial (cf. D.23.85 κρίσιν), and that undergoing trial was a way of avoiding *androlepsiai*, even before any *androlepsiai* had been made (cf. D.23.83 : πρό-τερον μὲν ὑποσχεῖν δίκας ἀξιοῖ [sc. ὁ νόμος], μετὰ ταῦτα δέ . . .· ἐὰν δὲ μηδέτερον τούτων ἐθέλωσι, "τὸ ἀνδρολήψιόν" φη-σιν "εἶναι"). Thebes (or whatever state it was) might choose to undergo trial, to prove that Thebes was not guilty of protecting the killer of an Athenian. How would Thebes undergo trial ? Presumably by sending to Athens some official representatives who would argue the innocence of Thebes before the Athenian court. (If the court found Thebes guilty, what kind of penalty could be imposed ? The law does not say. Possibly *androlepsiai* could then be made.)

Thus, if it was thought that Thebes was protecting the killer of an Athenian, the relatives of the killed man could demand that the Thebans either extradite the killer or show in a law-court that they were not harbouring him. If the Thebans did neither of these things, the relatives could seize three Thebans and hold them until one or other of these things was done.

In the account in *Lexeis Rhetorikai*, the expression δίκην ὑφέξοντας is applied to the three hostages, not to their fellow-citizens, and the lexicographer clearly means that the hostages are to undergo trial. Two explanations of this are possible. One is that, if *androlepsiai* were made and then the hostages' fellow-citizens still failed to respond to the demand that they should either extradite the killer or show that they were not harbouring him, the hostages might be tried and punished in the killer's place. The other is that the lexicographer (or his source) has misunderstood the phrase δίκας ὑπόσχωσιν in the law. I do not know which of these explanations is right.

The final problem about this law is : what does Polydeukes mean by saying that one who employed *androlepsia* unjustly was ' not unaccountable ' ? Presumably he means that such a person could be prosecuted, but we have no other information about the procedure by which this was done.

Until the trial was held, it was considered proper for the dead person's family not to associate in any friendly manner with the person whom they accused of being the killer. This too is illustrated by the passage of the speech *On the Chorister* in which the khoregos alleges that Philokrates and the other members of Diodotos's family did not really believe him responsible for the death of Diodotos.

Ant.6.39-40. συνῆσάν μοι καὶ διελέγοντο ἐν τοῖς ἱεροῖς, ἐν τῇ ἀγορᾷ, ἐν τῇ ἐμῇ οἰκίᾳ, ἐν τῇ σφετέρᾳ αὐτῶν, καὶ ἑτέρωθι πανταχοῦ. τὸ τελευταῖον, ὦ Ζεῦ καὶ θεοὶ πάντες, Φιλοκράτης αὐτὸς οὑτοσὶ ἐν τῷ βουλευτηρίῳ ἐναντίον τῆς βουλῆς, ἑστὼς μετ' ἐμοῦ ἐπὶ τοῦ βήματος, ἁπτόμενος ἐμοῦ διελέγετο, ὀνόματι οὗτος ἐμὲ προσαγορεύων, καὶ ἐγὼ τοῦτον, ὥστε δεινὸν δόξαι εἶναι τῇ βουλῇ, ἐπειδὴ ἐπύθετο προειρημένον μοι εἴργεσθαι τῶν νομίμων ὑπὸ τούτων οὓς ἑώρων μοι τῇ προτεραίᾳ συνόντας καὶ διαλεγομένους. 'They met me and conversed with me in the holy places, in the agora, in my house, in theirs, and everywhere else. Why, God Almighty ! this man Philokrates himself stood with me on

the platform in the council-house, with the council look-
ing on ; he touched me and talked with me, he addressing
me by name and I him. So the council thought it extra-
ordinary when they heard that a proclamation had been
made to me to keep away from the legal things, by people
whom they saw meeting me and conversing with me on
the previous day.'

The family was a unit. The whole family was offended by
the killing of one of its members. The whole family had
to take action against the killer, and regarded him as an
enemy.

III

THE BASILEUS

THE basileus, or 'king', was the official in charge of all homicide cases. The way in which this official evolved from the hereditary kings of prehistoric Athens need not be discussed here ; in the classical period he was no longer a king in any ordinary sense. He was appointed for one year only, to perform certain specified functions, and ranked as second in importance of ' the nine arkhons '.

The method of appointment of all the nine arkhons until 487 was election. (Arist.*Pol.*1274a1-2, 15-17 gives election as the method of appointment both before and after the reforms of Solon. In *Ath.Pol.*8.1 it is stated that Solon introduced the use of lot into the appointment of the arkhons, but this may be a mistake; see the discussion in Hignett 321-6.) But in 487/6 the system was changed to κλήρωσις ἐκ προκρίτων, appointment by lot out of a number of candidates previously selected (*Ath.Pol.*22.5). The Athenian citizens, voting in their separate demes, elected five hundred candidates (that is, each of the ten tribes elected fifty) ; from these five hundred the nine arkhons were chosen by lot. This method was still in use in 457 (*Ath.Pol.* 26.2), but at some later date the system was changed again and arkhons were henceforth appointed entirely by lot (*Ath.Pol.*8.1, 55.1). Thus it could not be expected that the persons appointed would have any particular ability, knowledge, or other qualifications. When Theogenes became basileus, he was ' inexperienced in affairs ' (D.59.72). The

33

presiding officer in homicide courts was essentially a layman, not a specialist.

The basileus was 'in charge of the most important matters' (Lys.26.11). Most of his duties were connected with religion. For example, he was at the head of the organization of almost all state sacrifices, and of processions and contests of various kinds at various religious festivals (*Ath.Pol.*57.1), and he supervised leases of sacred land (*Ath.Pol.*47.4). He took charge of legal cases concerned with religious offences, such as sacrilege or impiety (ἀσέβεια) and false claims to a priesthood (And.1.111, D.22.27, 35.48, *Ath.Pol.*57.2).

It was not the duty of the basileus to initiate a prosecution for homicide. As I have explained in chapter II, the first step had to be taken by the accuser, normally the relatives of the killed person or the master of a killed slave, who made application to the basileus. For ' make application ' or ' prefer a charge ' or ' obtain leave to bring a case ' two verbs are used, ἀπογράφεσθαι (e.g. Ant.6.35-46) and λαγχάνειν (e.g. D.47.69); but we cannot tell whether the two verbs are used simply as synonyms or refer to different, though closely connected, actions, since we have no details about this stage of the procedure.

The basileus made a proclamation against the person accused of homicide (*Ath.Pol.*57.2, Polyd.8.90, *Lexeis Rhetorikai* in *Lex.Seg.*310.6-8 ; see pages 23-6). His next task was to hold three *prodikasiai*, or ' pre-trials ', in three separate months, in preparation for the trial itself, which was held in the fourth month. All three *prodikasiai* and the final trial were conducted by the same basileus. Consequently the basileus would not accept a homicide charge in the last three months of his year of office (Mounikhion, Thargelion, and Skirophorion), because he had not enough time left to complete its hearing. At any rate, this is alleged by the khoregos. He maintains that the basileus of the preceding year acted quite properly in refusing to accept the charge brought by Philokrates for the killing of Diodotos.

Ant.6.42. ἔδει μὲν γὰρ τὸν βασιλέα, ἐπειδὴ ἀπεγράψατο, τρεῖς προδικασίας ποιῆσαι ἐν τρισὶ μησί, τὴν δίκην δ᾽ εἰσάγειν τετάρτῳ μηνί, ὥσπερ νυνί· τῆς δ᾽ ἀρχῆς αὐτῷ λοιποὶ δύο μῆνες ἦσαν, Θαργηλιὼν καὶ Σκιροφοριών. καὶ οὔτ᾽ εἰσάγειν δήπου οἷός τ᾽ ἂν ἦν ἐφ᾽ ἑαυτοῦ, οὔτε παραδοῦναι φόνου δίκην ἔξεστιν, οὐδὲ παρέδωκεν οὐδεὶς πώποτε βασιλεὺς ἐν τῇ γῇ ταύτῃ. ἥντινα οὖν μήτε εἰσάγειν μήτε παραδοῦναι ἐξῆν αὐτῷ, οὐδ᾽ ἀπογράφεσθαι ἠξίου παρὰ τοὺς ὑμετέρους νόμους. 'After accepting the charge, the basileus had to hold three *prodikasiai* in three months and bring the case to trial in a fourth month (as has now been done). But only two months of his term of office remained, Thargelion and Skirophorion. So you see he could not have brought it to trial in his own term of office ; and it is not permitted to pass on a case of homicide to a successor, nor has any basileus in this country ever done so. Since therefore he was permitted neither to bring it to trial nor to pass it on, he decided not to accept the charge at all in contravention of the laws of Athens.'

It is suggested by ten Berge 283-5 that the basileus could have accepted the charge if he had wished, even though not enough of his term of office remained for the case to come to trial. This may be true. But it is unlikely to be true that the basileus was legally required to accept a charge in such circumstances (as the accusers of the khoregos seem to have alleged) ; for then Philokrates, Philinos, and the others would surely have pressed their charge and raised an outcry against him either immediately or at his *euthynai* (cf. Ant.6.43), and not merely at the trial in the following year. So we may believe that the basileus was not legally required to accept a homicide charge in the last three months of his term of office. If any reader thinks that to delay a homicide charge for up to three months just because it happened to arise at a certain time of year is too absurd an arrangement to have been employed by a civilized society, let him consider the delay caused to a case for trial in an English county court if it is just too late for one session of assizes, or the fate of a bill at Westminster introduced too late in the Parliamentary session for all its stages to be completed.

What happened at the *prodikasiai*? The late lexicons have explanations of the term.

Photios (and Souda). προδικασία· οἱ τὰς ἐπὶ φόνῳ δίκας ἐγκαλούμενοι ἐν πρυτανείῳ πρὸ τῆς δίκης διατελοῦσιν ἐπὶ τρεῖς μῆνας· ἐν οἷς ἐξ ἑκατέρου μέρους λόγοι προάγονται. τοῦτό φασι προδικασίαν. 'Prodikasia: persons accused on charges of homicide live at the prytaneion for three months before the trial; in these months speeches are delivered on each side. This is called *prodikasia*.'

Dikon Onomata in *Lex.Seg.*186.21-3. ὅταν δὲ προγυμνάζηται ἡ δίκη πρὸ τῆς κυρίας, προδικασία λέγεται. 'When a practice trial is held before the principal one, it is called *prodikasia*.'

The lexicographers do not really explain what was the purpose of the *prodikasiai*. But it is fair to make some conjectures. They will have given the basileus an opportunity to learn what were the main features of the case, and thus which of the various homicide courts ought to try it (since the allocation of a case to a court depended on the nature of the accusation made and of the defence offered). They will have given the accused man an opportunity to hear the charges against him expounded in full, so that he could

make sure that his defence was adequate, decide what witnesses he needed to call, and so forth. They may sometimes
(though not always ; clearly not in the case of Kratinos,
described in Isok.18.52-4 and discussed on pages 53-4) have
given the prosecutor a chance to hear what line of defence
the accused man was likely to adopt. And if in this way
either party discovered that his opponent's case was too
strong to be refuted, the *prodikasiai* may sometimes even
have made it unnecessary to hold the final trial at all.

The prytaneion was a building on the northern side of the
akropolis, used for various official purposes. There is no
other evidence either to confirm or to refute the statement
(Photios and Souda προδικασία) that persons accused of
homicide lived there until the trial.

After the *prodikasiai* the basileus brought the case to its
final trial ; the verb used for this is εἰσάγειν. This means
that he fixed the date and place, and made arrangements for
the attendance of the appropriate jury. At the trial he no
doubt presided and told the parties when to speak or stop
speaking, but, like the arkhons presiding in other kinds of
case, did not sum up or advise the jury in any way. But
was the basileus himself a member of the jury ? In *Ath.Pol.*
57.4 we read: ὁ βασιλεὺς ὅταν δικάζῃ περιαιρεῖται τὸν στέφανον,
' when the basileus judges, he removes his crown '. The
most interesting thing in this statement is not the ceremonial
uncovering but the use of the verb δικάζειν, ' judge '. As a
rule, the jury is said to judge a case ; the presiding arkhon
merely brings it in (εἰσάγειν). Again, an orator speaks of
the basileus as ' judging cases of homicide ' (Lys.26.12 : φόνου δίκας δικάζοντα), and a similar expression is used in the
decree of Patrokleides (And.1.78). Lipsius 17-18 suggests
that the use of the verb ' judge ' implies that the basileus
had a vote, as a member of the jury, unlike the presiding

arkhon in other kinds of case. In support of this view he quotes also a passage from the law about unintentional homicide, *IG* i² 115.11-13: [δ]ικάζεν δὲ τὸς βασιλέας . . .· τὸς [δ]ὲ ἐφέτας διαγν[ῶναι], ' the basileis are to judge . . .; and the ephetai are to decide '. But this rather strange sentence is in fact evidence against Lipsius's view, not for it. True, the verb δικάζειν is used of the basileus (or ' the basileis ' ; the problem of why the plural is used is discussed on pages 87-8), but it cannot mean that the basileus is to decide the case, because it is specifically stated that it is the ephetai who are to do that. Thus this sentence is evidence that δικάζειν, with the basileus as subject, may mean something different from ' decide '. But what ? (Various senses of δικάζειν are discussed by J. H. Kells in *CQ* x [1960] 129-134, but not its use in connexion with the basileus.) I suggest that perhaps what the basileus did was to preside over the trial and at the end make a formal pronouncement, in accordance with the decision reached by the ephetai, that the accused was guilty or not guilty, and that the word δικάζειν may have been used for these functions. (Cf. Wolff 75-6. In a rather similar way the presiding officer at an English trial by jury is called ' the judge ' and is said to ' try ' the case, even though he does not decide the verdict.) This interpretation would fit all the relevant passages (*IG* i² 115.11-13, And.1.78, Lys.26.12, *Ath.Pol.*57.4). It is only a possible interpretation, not a certain one ; nevertheless it is clear that these passages are not adequate evidence that the basileus was a member of the jury and had a vote.

The verdict in homicide cases depended, then, not on the basileus, but on the Areopagos or the ephetai who formed the jury in the various courts.

IV

THE AREOPAGOS

THE council of the Areopagos was so called because from early times it met on the hill of Ares ("Αρειος πάγος), west of the akropolis. In the fourth century it met sometimes at the basileios stoa, at the north-west of the agora (D.25.23), and H. A. Thompson has argued (in *Hesperia* xxii [1953] 51-3 ; cf. B. D. Meritt in *Hesperia* xxii 129) that at this period its normal meeting-place was the old bouleuterion, on the west side of the agora. However, the view which I think more likely (and which is admitted as an alternative possibility by Thompson in *Hesperia* xxii 53 note 52a; cf. R. E. Wycherley in *JHS* lxxv [1955] 118-21) is that the normal meeting-place in the fourth century remained the hill of Ares. There may have been a roofed hall for meetings; but if so, homicide trials were held outside it, since such trials were always conducted in the open air (Ant.5.11, *Ath.Pol.*57.4, Polyd.8.118).

The origin and early history of the Areopagos are shrouded in legend and obscurity. At one period it seems to have had extensive political powers, but many of these powers were lost before the opening of the fifth century, and most of those that remained were transferred to other bodies by the reform of Ephialtes in 462/1. From then onwards, though it occasionally took political action in times of emergency (e.g. Lys.12.69), its chief function was that of a law-court, and that function is the only one with which I am concerned here.

It was composed entirely of ex-arkhons. Each year the nine men who held the arkhonships automatically became members of the Areopagos, and this membership, alone of Athenian offices (as distinct from religious appointments), was held for life (*Ath.Pol.*3.6). In two places (D.24.22, *Ath.Pol.*60.3) we hear of rules that an arkhon had to perform some specified duty before ' going up to the Areopagos ', and Polyd.8.118 states definitely that the arkhons became Areopagites after undergoing their *euthynai*, the examinations of their conduct in office. This seems to prove that an arkhon became a member of the Areopagos at the end of the year of his arkhonship, not at the beginning. (The only evidence against this is Lys.7.22 : τοὺς ἐννέα ἄρχοντας ἢ ἄλλους τινὰς τῶν ἐξ 'Αρείου πάγου. At first sight this appears to mean ' the nine arkhons or some other members of the Areopagos ', implying that the arkhons were members. However, it may mean ' the nine arkhons, or else some members of the Areopagos ' ; in other words, ἄλλος may mean not that the arkhons were members of the Areopagos but that the members of the Areopagos were different persons from the arkhons. For this use of ἄλλος compare, for example, S.*OT* 7, X.*An.*1.5.5, *Kyr.*1.6.2, Pl.*Grg.*473d, Ais. 1.163, *Ath.Pol.*57.4. In this case, there is no objection to the view that arkhons became Areopagites only at the end of their arkhonship.)

An arkhon might be debarred from ' going up to the Areopagos ' if he had failed to perform properly the functions of his arkhonship, and in such a case the ruling against him was made (at least in some instances) not by the Areopagos itself but by an ordinary law-court (D.26.5). Whether a man who had once become an Areopagite could be expelled from membership is not quite clear. We hear of one occasion on which the Areopagites forbade a man to ' go up to the Areopagos ' because he had breakfasted in a café (Hyp. fr.138 = Ath.566f). But he may have been excluded only from the meeting on that one day, and not permanently, and other passages which have sometimes been thought relevant to this question (D.54.25, Dein.1.56) probably refer to the expulsion of an ordinary Athenian from Attica rather than the expulsion of an Areopagite from the Areopagos. Strict rules were imposed on the members of the Areopagos to uphold its dignity; for example, they were forbidden to write comedies (Plu.*Ethika* 348c). They were also subject to *euthynai* (Ais.3.20), but we are not told whether any member was ever found guilty at this examination, or what kind of action counted as misconduct in office.

On these scraps of evidence about its membership we can base several conjectures about the character of the Areopagos as a jury. First, the Areopagites were all men with some legal experience. Every one of them had spent a year presiding, as one of the nine arkhons, over various law-courts (though of course only one-ninth of them, those who had held the office of basileus, had been concerned during that year with cases of homicide). This experience was perhaps the most important difference between the Areopagos and an ordinary heliastic jury. Secondly, the fact that they held office for life meant that their decisions were unlikely to be influenced by popular or official disapproval; an Areopagite voted as he liked (perhaps resembling in this a member of the House of Lords) without fear that he might be dismissed from office or might fail to be re-elected. In this respect the Areopagos was much like a heliastic jury. Thirdly, it was, by Athenian standards, a small jury. The number of men in a heliastic jury was commonly five hundred, sometimes more; in one case it is said to have been six thousand (And.1.17). The number of Areopagites will have varied according to their ages of appointment as arkhons and their longevity, but it can never have been as high as five hundred, and generally not much more than two hundred. So they will have been less subject than heliastic jurors to the dangers of mass emotion. Fourthly, they may have been easier to bribe than heliastic jurors. This is not only because they were fewer, but also because, whereas elaborate precautions were taken to prevent advance knowledge of which heliastic jurors would try which case (*Ath.Pol.*63-6), cases of homicide (of certain kinds) were bound to be tried by the Areopagos, and it was general knowledge which men were Areopagites. This greater possibility of corruption is perhaps the only respect in which the Areopagos was inferior to a heliastic jury. However, we never hear of any actual instance in which an Areopagite was even alleged (let alone proved) to have accepted a bribe; so possibly the Areopagos's traditional sense of responsibility was so strong that the danger of corruption was found in practice to be negligible.

On the whole, then, the Areopagos was probably the best jury in Athens. This was the opinion also of Sokrates (according to X.*Apom.*3.5.20), of Aiskhines (1.92), and of Lykourgos, who calls it the finest court in Greece: 'It is so far different from the other courts that even those who are convicted agree that their trials are just' (Lyk.12). Demosthenes concurs: 'This court alone neither tyrant nor oligarchy nor democracy has dared to deprive of homicide trials, but all believe that their own verdicts in these cases would be inferior to the verdicts of these men. That is remarkable enough; but in addition this is the only court where no accused man who was condemned or prosecutor who lost his case ever proved that the verdict was unjust' (D.23.66).

Demosthenes's words are a notable tribute. They show also that the competence of the Areopagos to try homicide cases lasted throughout the age of the orators. So when Lysias mentions τῷ δικαστηρίῳ τῷ ἐξ Ἀρείου πάγου, ᾧ καὶ πάτριόν ἐστι καὶ ἐφ' ἡμῶν ἀποδέδοται τοῦ φόνου τὰς δίκας δικάζειν, ' the court of the Areopagos, to which the trying of homicide cases traditionally belongs and also has been assigned in our own time ' (Lys.1.30), this must not be taken to imply that homicide trials were removed from the Areopagos at some earlier date and restored to it in the late fifth century. ἀποδέδοται may mean simply that this function was reaffirmed in some way, possibly in 409/8, when we know that at least part of the existing homicide law was reinscribed (*IG* i² 115).

The Areopagos tried legal cases on the three days preceding the last day of each month (Polyd.8.117 : τετάρτῃ φθίνοντος, τρίτῃ, δευτέρᾳ). Lucian says (*Hermotimos* 64) that it tried cases in the darkness of night (ἐν νυκτὶ καὶ σκότῳ δικάζουσιν) in order that the appearance of speakers might not distract attention from what they said ; but there is no other evidence that trials were nocturnal, and I suspect that Lucian either has made a mistake or is referring only to one or two exceptional occasions. Various parts of the procedure followed in homicide courts will be discussed in chapters X and XI. But it is worth mentioning here that the Areopagos had one special rule of its own. Speakers were forbidden to speak off the point (ἔξω τοῦ πράγματος λέγειν), and if anyone did so the herald stopped his speech (Lys.3.46, Lyk.12-13, Arist.*Rhet*.1354a22-3, Lucian *Anakharsis* 19). We are not told whether the herald decided for himself whether particular remarks were relevant, or how he received instructions to intervene. But the rule must certainly have discouraged the irrelevant pleadings and personal attacks which are a conspicuous feature of extant Athenian speeches delivered before other juries, and have helped the Areopagites to focus their attention on the true merits of the case.

The kinds of case tried in this court are defined in a law quoted in the speech *Against Aristokrates*.

D.23.22. δικάζειν δὲ τὴν βουλὴν τὴν ἐν Ἀρείῳ πάγῳ φόνου καὶ τραύματος ἐκ προνοίας καὶ πυρκαιᾶς καὶ φαρμάκων, ἐάν τις ἀποκτείνῃ δούς. 'The council on the Areopagos is to try cases of homicide and wounding committed deliberately and arson and poison, if anyone causes death by giving it.'

A list obviously based on this law is given in the *Ath.Pol.*

*Ath.Pol.*57.3. εἰσὶ δὲ φόνου δίκαι καὶ τραύματος, ἂν μὲν ἐκ προνοίας ἀποκτείνῃ ἢ τρώσῃ, ἐν Ἀρείῳ πάγῳ, καὶ φαρμάκων, ἐὰν ἀποκτείνῃ δούς, καὶ πυρκαιᾶς· ταῦτα γὰρ ἡ βουλὴ μόνα δικάζει. 'Trials for homicide and wounding, if the killing or wounding is committed deliberately, are held on the Areopagos ; so are those for poison, if one causes death by giving it, and arson. These are the only cases which the council tries.'

Since I am at present concerned only with homicide, I shall say nothing about the inclusion of arson and wounding in the list. Nor shall I discuss cases of the destruction of sacred olive-trees, which were tried by the Areopagos until some date in the fourth century (*Ath.Pol.*60.2 ; cf. Lys.7).

Three small problems are raised by the terminology of the law, but none causes much difficulty. One concerns the word δούς, 'by giving it'. Lipsius 124 maintains that this word means 'by administering it with one's own hand' (and a similar view is taken by ten Berge 166, commenting on Ant.6.15) ; it would thus be intended to exclude explicitly any person who merely ordered, persuaded, or assisted someone else to administer poison. I suspect that Lipsius draws more significance from the word than the author of the law intended it to have. But the point is unimportant, be cause there is also other evidence (see chapter VI) that cases of *bouleusis* ('complicity') were tried at the Palladion, not on the Areopagos. So whatever the significance of δούς, we can conclude that a poisoner was tried on the Areopagos only if he was accused of administering the poison himself.

Killing by poison is a kind of homicide. Why then is it mentioned separately from φόνος? Thiel (*Mnemosyne* II lvi 91-2) suggests that the word φόνος originally meant killing by violence and bloodshed, and that poison was mentioned specifically to make clear that it too was covered by the law and could not be committed with impunity; and this is probably correct. But by the time of the orators the mean- ing of φόνος had been extended to include poisoning. The persons accused of causing death by poison in the cases of Antiphon 1 and 6 (the stepmother and the khoregos) are both accused of φόνος; this shows that we need not dis- tinguish φόνος and φάρμακα as two separate kinds of charge.

The third problem concerns the expression ἐκ προνοίας, 'committed deliberately'. In the law as quoted by De- mosthenes, this phrase is placed with τραύματος, 'wounding'; is it meant to apply also to the other offences in the list? The answer must be yes; the way in which the author of the *Ath.Pol.* has reworded the law shows that he took it to refer to killing as well as wounding, and there is besides plenty of other evidence (see chapter VI) that cases of unintentional homicide were tried at the Palladion, not on the Areopagos. This means that the case went to the Palladion if the accuser, not merely the accused, said that the killing was uninten tional. If the accuser said that the killing was intentional, the case would go to the Areopagos, but the Areopagos might still decide that the killing was unintentional. The rule is illustrated by a case related by Aristotle.

Arist. *Ethika Megala* 1188b29-38. ὅταν γάρ τις πατάξῃ τινὰ ἢ ἀποκτείνῃ ἤ τι τῶν τοιούτων ποιήσῃ μηδὲν προδιανοηθείς, ἄκοντά φαμεν ποιῆσαι, ὡς τοῦ ἑκουσίου ὄντος ἐν τῷ διανοηθῆναι. οἷόν φασί ποτέ τινα γυναῖκα φίλτρον τινὶ δοῦναι πιεῖν, εἶτα τὸν ἄνθρωπον ἀποθανεῖν ὑπὸ τοῦ φίλτρου, τὴν δ' ἄνθρωπον ἐν Ἀρείῳ πάγῳ ἀποφυγεῖν· οὗ παροῦσαν δι' οὐθὲν ἄλλο ἀπέλυσαν ἢ διότι οὐκ ἐκ προνοίας. ἔδωκε μὲν γὰρ φιλίᾳ, διήμαρτεν δὲ τούτου· διὸ οὐχ ἑκούσιον ἐδόκει εἶναι, ὅτι τὴν δόσιν τοῦ φίλτρου οὐ μετὰ διανοίας τοῦ ἀπολέσθαι αὐτὸν ἐδίδου. ἐνταῦθα ἄρα τὸ ἑκούσιον πίπτει εἰς τὸ μετὰ διανοίας. 'Whenever a person hits another or kills him or does anything of that sort with no previous deliberation, we say that he did it unintentionally, on the ground that intention lies in deliberation. For instance, it is said that on one occasion a woman gave a man a love-philtre to drink, and afterwards he died from the philtre, but she was acquitted on the Areopagos, where they let off the accused woman for no other reason than that she did not do it deliberately. For she gave it to him for love, but she failed to achieve this aim; so they decided it was not intentional, because she did not give him the philtre with the thought of killing him. So here the intentional is classed with the deliberate.'

This example shows that the Areopagos did not convict persons for unintentional homicide. If it found them not guilty of intentional homicide, it simply acquitted them. They could not be convicted of unintentional homicide unless they were accused of it before the proper court, at the Palladion. (The contrary assertion of Lipsius 132 arises from the mistake of thinking that ἀποφυγεῖν in this passage refers to exile.) But besides this Aristotle's words are interesting because they illuminate one of the fundamental distinctions made in Athenian homicide law, the distinction between the intentional and the unintentional. Such a distinction is irrespective of the fate of the killed man, and it is also irrespective of the pollution incurred by the state from the shedding of blood. It thus has nothing to do with doctrines of vengeance and cleansing. It adapts the penalty for killing to the killer, and it takes into account not merely the killer's act but his attitude of mind.

On the whole, the kinds of homicide for which trials were held on the Areopagos were the ones which were considered the most serious. But these did not correspond at all exactly to the kinds which are regarded as murder in English law or in other modern legal systems, and for this reason it is better to avoid using the term ' murder ' in connexion with the Areopagos. Similarly ' manslaughter ' is not an adequate term for the kinds of homicide tried by the ephetai in their various courts, which have to be discussed next.

V

THE EPHETAI

THE name 'ephetai' is said by Harpokration (under ἐπὶ Παλλαδίῳ) to be derived from the verb ἐφίημι in its sense of 'refer'; the ephetai were persons to whom a case was referred. Polydeukes (8.125) gives a similar explanation. Modern scholars have alternative derivations: Lipsius 15 derives it from ἐφίεμαι in the sense of 'instruct' and translates it 'Anweiser des Rechts'; Bonner and Smith i 101 prefer to derive it from ἐφίεμαι as a passive and translate it 'men sent out as a commission'; and in note 2 on the same page they list a variety of other suggestions. But in any case the origin of the name is of no importance for understanding the activities of the ephetai in the fifth and fourth centuries. (A student of twentieth-century British officials would find an etymological study of 'Lord Privy Seal', for example, unhelpful, and of 'Speaker' positively misleading.) We must look at the evidence of what the ephetai actually did.

Harp. ἐφέται· . . . οἱ δικάζοντες τὰς ἐφ' αἵματι κρίσεις ἐπὶ Παλλαδίῳ καὶ ἐπὶ πρυτανείῳ καὶ ἐπὶ Δελφινίῳ καὶ ἐν Φρεαττοῖ ἐφέται ἐκαλοῦντο. 'Ephetai: the men who judged cases of homicide at the Palladion and at the prytaneion and at the Delphinion and in Phreatto were called "ephetai".'

Polyd.8.125. ἐφέται τὸν μὲν ἀριθμὸν εἷς καὶ πεντήκοντα, Δράκων δ' αὐτοὺς κατέστησεν ἀριστίνδην αἱρεθέντας·

ἐδίκαζον δὲ τοῖς ἐφ' αἵματι διωκομένοις ἐν τοῖς πέντε δικα-
στηρίοις. Σόλων δ' αὐτοῖς προσκατέστησε τὴν ἐξ 'Αρείου
πάγου βουλήν. 'The ephetai were fifty-one in number.
They were instituted by Drakon and appointed according
to rank. They tried men accused of homicide in their
five courts. Solon instituted in addition to them the
council of the Areopagos.'

Since Harpokration's work is a lexicon of terms used by
the Attic orators, it may be taken for granted that he is
referring here to the age of the orators, and not to some
earlier period. Polydeukes goes back to the time of Drakon,
but the origin of the ephetai is an insoluble problem with
which I do not intend to deal. For the period after Solon,
his remarks clearly imply what Harpokration explicitly
states, that the ephetai judged cases at the Palladion, at the
prytaneion, at the Delphinion, and in Phreatto.

It appears possible that the prytaneion is included in this
list by mistake ; I revert to this possibility in chapter IX.
But about the courts at the Palladion, at the Delphinion, and
in Phreatto, earlier evidence indicates that Harpokration's
statement is correct. IG i² 115 is an inscription of 409/8
containing a new copy of the law about unintentional homicide : such cases are judged by ℎοι πεντέκοντα καὶ ℎês ℎοι
ἐφέται, 'the fifty-one, the ephetai'. Most of these words are
lost in the inscription, but the restoration is guaranteed by
the quotation of the same law in D.43.57, which also indicates that the law was still in force in the time of Demosthenes. Laws quoted in And.1.78 (the decree of Patrokleides, of the year 405) and in D.23.37-8 also refer to the
judging of cases by the ephetai. In Ath.Pol.57.4 we read,
with reference to homicide cases : δικάζουσι δ' οἱ λαχόντες
ταῦ[τ' ἐφέται] πλὴν τῶν ἐν 'Αρείῳ πάγῳ γιγνομένων, 'these
cases, except those held on the Areopagos, are tried by the

ephetai who are appointed by lot'. The word 'ephetai' here is restored by Kenyon, but in view of the other evidence about the ephetai it need not be doubted.

The lexicographers offer a few further scraps of information.

Photios (and Souda). ἐφέται· ἄνδρες ὑπὲρ πεντήκοντα ἔτη γεγονότες καὶ ἄριστα βεβιωκέναι ὑπόληψιν ἔχοντες· οἳ καὶ τὰς φονικὰς δίκας ἔκρινον. 'Ephetai : men over the age of fifty and with a reputation for having lived virtuously. These were the men who tried homicide cases.' (Almost the same words appear in *Dikon Onomata* in *Lex.Seg.*188. 30-2.)

The statement that the ephetai were over the age of fifty is not contradicted by any other evidence, and may well be correct. The statement that they had a reputation for virtuous living is more doubtful. If it implies that virtue was the criterion by which ephetai were selected, it seems to contradict the statement of *Ath.Pol.*57.4 that they were appointed by lot. Either the lexicographers are referring to a different (probably earlier) period from the *Ath.Pol.*; or the system was that fifty-one ephetai were appointed by lot out of a larger number previously selected for their virtuous lives ; or else (and this is the likeliest explanation) the lexicographers have simply misunderstood the statement of *Polyd.*8.125 that in the time of Drakon the ephetai were appointed ἀριστίνδην, 'according to rank', and we should conclude that in early times, when Athens was still governed by an aristocracy, the ephetai were aristocrats, but later, under the democracy, they were appointed by lot (just as the arkhons in early times were aristocrats but after 487/6 were appointed by lot).

There is also some contradictory evidence about the number of the ephetai. Passages which I have already mentioned (*IG* i² 115, D.43.57, Polyd.8.125) say that they were fifty-one in number. But one of the entries in the Souda lexicon under ἐφέται states that they were eighty : π' ὄντες. The lexicon of Zonaras under ἐφέται (page 926 in Tittmann's edition) also gives the number as eighty, but doubtless this statement comes from the same source and cannot be regarded as independent testimony. However, Photios, giving the same entry as we find in the Souda, has a different reading at this point : the manuscript gives περι-όντες, ' surviving ', which was emended by Porson to περι-ιόντες, ' going on circuit '. I do not know what was originally written by the authority on whom these lexico-graphers drew, but clearly their statements are too confused to be used to contradict our other evidence that the number of the ephetai was fifty-one. For the same reason the state-ment of Timaios, under ἐφέται in his Platonic lexicon, that the number was fifty can be dismissed as an inaccurate approximation.

A more difficult question is whether the ephetai were mem-bers of the Areopagos. Whereas Jones 259-60 says that they were not, Bonner and Smith i 99-100 maintain that they were, quoting as evidence fragments of Androtion and Philokhoros.

FGrH 324 F4a, 328 F20b. ἐκ γὰρ τῶν ἐννέα καθιστα-μένων ἀρχόντων 'Αθήνησι τοὺς 'Αρεοπαγίτας ἔδει συν-εστάναι δικαστάς, ὥς φησιν 'Ανδροτίων ἐν δευτέρᾳ τῶν 'Ατθίδων· ὕστερον δὲ πλειόνων γέγονεν ἡ ἐξ 'Αρείου πάγου βουλή, τουτέστιν ἡ ἐξ ἀνδρῶν περιφανεστέρων πεντήκοντα καὶ ἑνός, πλὴν ἐξ εὐπατριδῶν, ὡς ἔφημεν, καὶ πλούτῳ καὶ βίῳ σώφρονι διαφερόντων, ὡς ἱστορεῖ Φιλόχορος διὰ τῆς τρίτης τῶν αὐτοῦ 'Ατθίδων. ' At Athens the Areopagite judges had to be drawn from the nine men who were ap-pointed arkhons, as Androtion says in his second *Atthis*. Later the council of the Areopagos was formed from a larger number—that is, the council of fifty-one, composed of eminent men, but only of eupatrids, as we said, and men distinguished for wealth and sober life, as Philokhoros records in his third *Atthis*.'

This account is certainly muddled, since fifty-one would be a smaller number, not a larger number, than the total of men alive at any one time who had held one of the nine arkhonships. Nevertheless, it has been thought to show that the fifty-one ephetai were members of the Areopagos. J. W. Headlam (*CR* vi [1892] 251) says : ' We get however a clear distinction between 'Αρεοπαγῖται δικασταί and ἡ ἐξ 'Αρείου πάγου βουλή. The δικασταί would be the πεντήκοντα καὶ εἷς.' Bonner and Smith i 100 take a similar line. But to me it is by no means clear that a distinction is being made between ' the Areopagite judges ' and ' the council of the Areopagos '. The passage may mean only that at first the Areopagos was small, but later it was enlarged to a total of fifty-one ; and if so, it provides no information whatever about the ephetai. And since we have no other relevant evidence, the conclusion must be that we do not know whether the ephetai were members of the Areopagos or not.

Many scholars have believed that by the end of the fifth century the fifty-one ephetai had been superseded by larger juries of ordinary heliastai. Gertrude Smith (*CP* xix 353-8) argues that this change was made in the time of Perikles ; others have placed it in 409 or 403. Fourth-century references to ephetai are explained by assuming that the heliastai sitting in any of the homicide courts were given the name ' ephetai '. The chief obstacle to this view is that the expression ' the fifty-one, the ephetai ' occurs in the law about unintentional homicide already quoted, not only in the inscription of 409/8 (*IG* i² 115) but also in the quotation in a fourth-century speech (D.43.57). Miss Smith suggests that in the fourth century a body of fifty-one ephetai continued in existence for the sole purpose of granting pardon to exiled killers, while cases of homicide were tried by heliastai, also with the title ' ephetai '. But it is unlikely that two distinct bodies would each be known as ' *the* ephetai ' (the definite article is used in *IG* i² 115, And.1.78, D.23.37-8, 43.57). It is more likely that the fifty-one ephetai continued to function as a jury throughout the fourth century.

The view that they were superseded by juries of ordinary heliastai is based mainly on two passages. The speech of Isokrates *Against Kallimakhos* describes one of the few recorded cases in which the jury gave a unanimous verdict. The speaker tells the story, which is otherwise quite irrelevant to his own case, in order to illustrate Kallimakhos's dishonesty and so discredit him. A dispute arose between Kallimakhos's brother-in-law and Kratinos over the ownership of a piece of land. The quarrel led to blows, and after the fight Kallimakhos and his brother-in-law hid away a slave-woman, and then alleged that she had died from wounds inflicted by Kratinos and prosecuted him for homicide. The case was tried at the Palladion. The brother-in-law was the prosecutor, and Kallimakhos a witness that Kratinos had killed the woman. Kratinos and his supporters seized the woman by force from the house where she was hidden and exhibited her alive in court.

Isok.18.54. ὥσθ' ἑπτακοσίων μὲν δικαζόντων, τεττάρων δὲ καὶ δέκα μαρτυρησάντων ἅπερ οὗτος, οὐδεμίαν ψῆφον μετέλαβε. 'So in a court of seven hundred jurors, although fourteen witnesses had given the same evidence as he, he got not one vote.'

Most scholars take it for granted that this sentence describes the verdict in the homicide trial at the Palladion, and that it proves that the jury in the homicide trial was not fifty-one ephetai but seven hundred heliastai. But this interpretation is not entirely satisfactory. If Kallimakhos was so flagrantly guilty of lying, why was he not prosecuted for it by a charge for giving false evidence (δίκη ψευδομαρτυριῶν)? Or if he was tried on this charge, why does the speaker not gleefully relate the result of the trial ? And why does he say that Kallimakhos got no votes in the homicide trial, when the prosecutor in that trial was not Kallimakhos but his brother-in-law ?

It seems likely that Isokrates has telescoped the story. What probably happened is that Kallimakhos's evidence was so blatantly untrue that he was prosecuted for giving false evidence and was unanimously convicted by the jury. The account is condensed, partly because the speaker wishes only to narrate those parts of the affair which were discreditable to Kallimakhos, and has no interest in the verdict against his brother-in-law, and partly because any obscurities in his narrative would anyway be clarified for his hearers by the witnesses whom he calls immediately afterwards. If this is right, the seven hundred heliastai were not the jury at the Palladion but the jury which found Kallimakhos guilty of giving false evidence, and the passage does not prove that the ephetai had ceased to try homicide cases.

A rather similar case is described in the speech *Against Neaira*. The speaker wishes to discredit Stephanos. Stephanos, he says, alleged that Apollodoros went to Aphidna in search of a runaway slave, and in the course of the search struck a woman (presumably a slave of Stephanos, though this is not explicitly stated) who afterwards died from the blow. Stephanos prosecuted Apollodoros at the Palladion for homicide, and swore the oath that Apollodoros had killed the woman with his own hand.

D.59.10. ἐξελεγχθεὶς δ' ἐπιορκῶν καὶ ψευδῆ αἰτίαν ἐπι-
φέρων, καὶ καταφανὴς γενόμενος μεμισθωμένος ὑπὸ Κηφι-
σοφῶντος καὶ 'Απολλοφάνους ὥστ' ἐξελάσαι 'Απολλόδωρον
ἢ ἀτιμῶσαι ἀργύριον εἰληφώς, ὀλίγας ψήφους μεταλαβὼν
ἐκ πεντακοσίων δραχμῶν, ἀπῆλθεν ἐπιωρκηκὼς καὶ δόξας
πονηρὸς εἶναι. ' When it was proved that he had perjured
himself and the charge he had brought was false, and it
became obvious that he had been hired by Kephisophon
and Apollophanes, to banish or disfranchise Apollodoros
in return for money, he got few votes out of five hundred
drakhmai, and left the court, having become a perjurer
and acquired a bad reputation.'

' Out of five hundred drakhmai ' is an obscure phrase.
Does it refer to the money just mentioned (ἀργύριον), so
that the speaker means that after receiving five hundred
drakhmai to get Apollodoros condemned Stephanos man-
aged to get only a few votes cast against him ? Or does it
refer to money paid out by Stephanos, implying that he
spent five hundred drakhmai on the trial, on getting witnesses together (cf. D.59.9 παρασκευασάμενος, ' suborning ')
and perhaps also on bribing the jury, and got only a few
votes in return for his money ? Either interpretation seems
possible. But most editors simply delete δραχμῶν and take
the phrase as ' he got few votes out of five hundred ',
implying that five hundred jurors tried the case. This dele-
tion is not justified. It has not been proved that the reading
δραχμῶν is incorrect, nor that a case at the Palladion could
have been tried by five hundred jurors. It is still less justifiable to use the text thus emended as a principal witness for
the view that cases were no longer tried by the fifty-one
ephetai.

Other passages sometimes quoted in this connexion are
not much help. Nothing is proved by the fact that the

E

khoregos, defending himself at the Palladion, begins his speech by addressing the jury as ἄνδρες δικασταί (Ant.6.1). The word δικαστής may be applied to anyone who tries a case. If Demosthenes can use the term δικασταί of the twelve gods trying the case of Orestes on the Areopagos (D.23.66), there is no reason why it should not be used also of the fifty-one ephetai. Still less does the expression ὦ Ἀθηναῖοι in Lys.1.6-7 (spoken at the Delphinion) show, as Miss Smith suggests (CP xix 354), that the jury were not the fifty-one ephetai. Later in the same speech the jury's vote is said to be 'the most powerful of everything in the city' (Lys.1.36); but since the sentence contains a contrast between the jury's vote and the laws (τοὺς μὲν νόμους . . . τὴν δὲ ψῆφον τὴν ὑμετέραν . . .) it is clear that the speaker's point is simply that juries' verdicts can overrule laws, and he does not imply anything about the constitution of this particular jury. Nor is anything proved by the fact that in Ant.5.90 and D.47.73 the speaker, addressing a jury of heliastai, refers to the jury in a prospective homicide trial as 'you', since there 'you' simply means 'Athens', 'a jury representing you Athenians'. (For this use of 'you', cf. And.1.13; and see Maidment 225 note a, and my Andokides: On the Mysteries 66.)

There is thus no adequate reason to doubt that the fifty-one ephetai continued to function as a jury in the late fifth and in the fourth centuries, in accordance with references to them in extant laws of that period (IG i² 115, And.1.78, D.23.37-8, 43.57), or to believe that they were superseded by heliastic jurors.

The unsatisfactory and incomplete nature of the evidence about the ephetai makes it hard to estimate their virtues as a jury. But it does seem likely that they were superior to heliastic juries in at least one or two ways. They were men of experience (if it is true that they were all over fifty years of age)—experience of life, at any rate, even if not of law. Their small number will have made them less susceptible to mass emotion even than the Areopagos. Whether it also made them easier to bribe we cannot say, because we do not know how the lot was used in their appointment; if they were selected by lot only just before the trial began, corruption may have been effectively prevented. There is no reason to suppose that the ephetai were not an efficient and impartial jury.

VI

THE PALLADION

THE Palladion, from its name, was clearly a temple of Pallas
Athena, though it seems that not only was Athena wor-
shipped there (*IG* i² 324 lines 78 and 95), but also Zeus (*IG*
ii² 1096, 3177, 5055). Its situation is not clearly stated by
any ancient author, but in a fragment of Kleidemos (*FGrH*
323 F18=Plu.*Thes*.27.3-5) it is associated with Ardettos, a
hill south-east of Athens, not far outside the city wall. (The
story related by Paus.1.28.9 also implies that the Palladion
was outside the city. Cf. Walther Judeich *Topographie von
Athen*² 421.) Homicide trials will have been held outside the
temple, not inside, since all homicide courts sat in the open
air (Ant.5.11, *Ath.Pol*.57.4, Polyd.8.118); that is doubtless
why the court is always said to be 'at' (ἐπί) the Palladion,
not in it.

The kinds of case heard here are listed in the *Ath.Pol.*

*Ath.Pol.*57.3. τῶν δ' ἀκουσίων [sc. φόνων δίκας] καὶ
βουλεύσεως κἂν οἰκέτην ἀποκτείνῃ τις ἢ μέτοικον ἢ ξένον,
οἱ ἐπὶ Παλλαδίῳ [sc. δικάζουσιν]. 'Cases of unintentional
homicide and of *bouleusis* and anyone who kills a slave or
a metic or a foreigner are tried by the court at the Palladion.'

Demosthenes (23.71) also says that cases of unintentional
homicide were tried at the Palladion, and the fact is illustrated by a snatch of facetious dialogue surviving from a
lost play of Aristophanes.

Ar.fr.585.

" ἄκων κτενῶ σε, τέκνον." ὁ δ' ὑπεκρίνετο,
" ἐπὶ Παλλαδίῳ τἄρ', ὦ πάτερ, δώσεις δίκην ".
' " I shall kill you, my lad, without meaning to." The
boy replied, " In that case, father, you'll be punished for
it at the Palladion ".'

The law about unintentional homicide (*IG* i² 115, quoted
on pages 118-19) does not mention the Palladion, though it
does say that such cases are to be decided by the ephetai.
It uses the expression μὲ 'κ προνοίας, ' not from forethought ',
as a synonym for ' unintentionally ', but it makes no attempt
to define these terms further or to state precisely the important distinction between intentional and unintentional homicide. There are however two individual cases which help
to make the distinction clearer. First there is the example
given by Aristotle (*Ethika Megala* 1188b29-38, quoted on
page 46) of a man who died from a love-philtre which a
woman gave him. The Areopagos decided that she was
guilty only of unintentional homicide. She gave him the
philtre deliberately, but she did not intend death to be the
result. The second example is in the speech *Against Konon*,
written by Demosthenes for delivery by Ariston. Ariston
claims that Konon assaulted and injured him. He recovered,
but in the course of his speech he says that if he had died
from the injuries Konon would have been liable to be prosecuted for homicide (D.54.25) and would have been tried on
the Areopagos (D.54.28). This means that the charge
would have been one of intentional homicide. Yet, though
Ariston (or rather Demosthenes) does not mince his words
about Konon, nowhere in the speech does he allege that
Konon actually intended to kill him. So it is not true to say
that homicide was intentional only if the person responsible
intended death to be the result of his act. And it is equally

untrue (as Aristotle's example shows) to say that homicide was intentional whenever the person responsible intentionally performed the act which resulted in death. The truth must lie somewhere between these two. The rule may have been, for example, that homicide was intentional whenever death resulted from an act which was intended to cause harm. But unfortunately there are no other recorded cases which help us to discover whether this was actually the rule, or even whether the rule was ever precisely formulated.

Cases of *bouleusis* were also tried at the Palladion. The literal meaning of the word *bouleusis* is ' planning ', and its literary (as distinct from its legal) use is wide. A plan may be connected with homicide in a number of different ways. A plan may be made to kill someone, and it may either succeed or fail. A plan may be made to do something else, and may result in someone's death, although this was not the intention of the planner. A plan may be carried out by the person (or persons) who made it, or by someone else, or not at all. So quite a long list can be made of persons of whom a writer may use the verb βουλεύειν in connexion with homicide.

A : a person who plans to kill someone, and does so. E.g. S.*Tr*.807-8 (addressed to Deianeira) : τοιαῦτα, μῆτερ, πατρὶ βουλεύσασ᾽ ἐμῷ καὶ δρῶσ᾽ ἐλήφθης.

B : a person who makes a plan to kill, which is successfully carried out by someone else. E.g. A.*Ag*.1634-5 (addressed to Aigisthos) : ἐπειδὴ τῷδ᾽ ἐβούλευσας μόρον, δρᾶσαι τόδ᾽ ἔργον οὐκ ἔτλης αὐτοκτόνως.

C : a person who plans and carries out an act which is not intended to kill but does. E.g. in Ant.4c.4 a man who struck a blow which killed another is called βουλευτὴς τοῦ θανάτου, although μείζω ὧν ἤθελε πράξας.

D : a person who plans an act carried out by someone

else, which is not intended to kill but does. E.g. Ant.6.16-19 (spoken by the khoregos): διωμόσαντο δὲ οὗτοι μὲν ἀποκτεῖναί με Διόδοτον βουλεύσαντα τὸν θάνατον . . . αὐτοὶ οἱ κατήγοροι ὁμολογοῦσι μὴ ἐκ προνοίας μηδ' ἐκ παρασκευῆς γενέσθαι τὸν θάνατον τῷ παιδί.

E: a person who makes a plan to kill, which is not carried out at all. E.g. Hdt.5.92γ.2-3 (the plot to kill the infant Kypselos): ἐβεβούλευτο κατ' ὁδὸν τὸν πρῶτον αὐτῶν λαβόντα [sc. τὸ παιδίον] προσουδίσαι. . . . διεξῆλθε διὰ πάντων τῶν δέκα παραδιδόμενον, οὐδενὸς βουλομένου διεργάσασθαι.

F: a person who makes a plan to kill, which is carried out but does not succeed. E.g. Lys.3.42: ὅσοι ἐπιβουλεύσαντες ἀποκτεῖναί τινας ἔτρωσαν, ἀποκτεῖναι δὲ οὐκ ἐδυνήθησαν, περὶ τῶν τοιούτων τὰς τιμωρίας οὕτω μεγάλας κατεστήσαντο, ἡγούμενοι, ὑπὲρ ὧν ἐβούλευσαν καὶ προὐνοήθησαν, ὑπὲρ τούτων προσήκειν αὐτοῖς δίκην δοῦναι.

But the legal use of the term *bouleusis* is narrower than this, because some of these kinds of person were subject to other kinds of accusation. In law, obviously *A* would be accused simply of intentional homicide, and *C* of unintentional homicide (or possibly of intentional homicide, if his act was intended to cause harm; cf. pages 59-60). *F* might be accused of deliberate wounding (τραῦμα ἐκ προνοίας), as the speaker says in Lys.3 (though he doubtless exaggerates when he maintains that this was the only kind of person against whom such a charge might be brought). *E* might well not be prosecuted at all. However, it is not quite certain that *E* or *F* or both could not be prosecuted for *bouleusis* of homicide; Harpokration says that they could (βουλεύσεως· . . . ὅταν ἐξ ἐπιβουλῆς τίς τινι κατασκευάσῃ θάνατον, ἐάν τε ἀποθάνῃ ὁ ἐπιβουλευθεὶς ἐάν τε μή, copied in *Lexeis Rhetorikai* in *Lex.Seg.*220.12-14), and this possibility is admitted (rightly) by Maschke 89 and ten Berge 179, and even claimed (wrongly) as the only legal meaning of *bouleusis* by Treston 224-5 and Thiel (*Mnemosyne* II lvi 89-91).

But *B* and *D* clearly deserve to be prosecuted, and could not be prosecuted on other grounds ; so it was to these that charges of *bouleusis* of homicide were more or less confined. *B*'s offence was *bouleusis* of intentional homicide, *D*'s *bouleusis* of unintentional homicide. In each case the person who made the plan may be distinguished from the person who carried it out, and so in legal contexts we several times find βουλεύσας contrasted with χειρί or αὐτόχειρ, ' with one's own hand ' (Ant.6.16, And.1.94, Pl.*Laws* 871e-872b ; cf. Arist.*Rhet.*1364a19-23).

Good examples of cases of *bouleusis* of intentional and of unintentional homicide are provided by two speeches of Antiphon, both concerned with cases of poisoning. In Antiphon 1 (*Against the Stepmother*) the speaker is the dead man's illegitimate son. He is prosecuting the dead man's wife, his own stepmother, who is defended by her sons, the prosecutor's half-brothers. His father had a friend named Philoneos, and Philoneos had a slave-concubine, of whom he was tiring. His father's wife (alleges the prosecutor) told the slave-girl that she possessed a love-philtre which would increase the two men's affection for the slave-girl and herself, and they made a plan by which the speaker's stepmother was to provide the potion and the slave-girl was to put it in the wine when the two men were drinking together. An opportunity was found when Philoneos was entertaining the speaker's father at his house in Peiraieus. The girl put the potion in the wine, inserting a rather larger share in Philoneos's cup. Philoneos died at once. The speaker's father fell ill, and died some twenty days later. The slave-girl was executed. Now, some years afterwards, the speaker prosecutes his father's wife for killing his father. He claims that she caused his death deliberately, and the language he uses (e.g. Ant.1.26: ἑκουσίως καὶ βουλεύσασα) makes it clear that the charge is one of *bouleusis* of intentional homicide.

Antiphon 6 (*On the Chorister*) is a speech for the defence. The speaker was the khoregos for a boys' chorus at the festival of the Thargelia. In the course of the rehearsals one of the boys, named Diodotos, took some kind of drink, the nature of which is not explained anywhere in the speech, and soon afterwards died. The speaker is accused of causing the death of Diodotos by poison. His defence is that he did not attend the rehearsals himself, owing to pressure of other business, but appointed four men, including his own son-in-law Phanostratos, to act as his deputies and manage the chorus for Pantakles, who was the author and director of the performance (διδάσκαλος); so far from giving the boy the drink or ordering him to take it, he was not even present at the time. However, he does not put the blame on Phanostratos or any of the others; he attributes the boy's death simply to chance (Ant.6.15: τῆς τύχης). This defence may be thought a weak one. But I am not here concerned with the plausibility of the defence, but with the nature of the accusation. The use of the term βουλεύσας in the oath sworn by the accusers makes it certain that the khoregos was charged with *bouleusis*, not with poisoning ' with his own hand ' (Ant.6.16: διωμόσαντο δὲ οὗτοι μὲν ἀποκτεῖναί με Διόδοτον βουλεύσαντα τὸν θάνατον, ἐγὼ δὲ μὴ ἀποκτεῖναι, μήτε χειρὶ ἀράμενος [ἐργασάμενος Dobree] μήτε βουλεύσας). It is also explicitly stated that the prosecutors themselves agree that the boy's death was not caused deliberately (Ant. 6. 19: μὴ ἐκ προνοίας μηδ' ἐκ παρασκευῆς). So it is certain that the offence alleged is participation in an act which resulted in death although no harm was intended: the charge is one of *bouleusis* of unintentional homicide.

Nevertheless, the khoregos frequently mentions that he is accused of ' killing ' Diodotos, and that the charge is one of φόνος (notice especially Ant.6.36 : φόνου δίκην). So there is no doubt that such expressions as ' killing ' and ' homicide ' were used even when a case was merely one of *bouleusis* of unintentional homicide. (This undermines the argument of Gernet *Antiphon* 33-4, that because the speaker of Ant.1 accuses his stepmother of φόνος the charge against her was not one of *bouleusis*. Thiel, in *Mnemosyne* II lvi 87-91, and Wijnberg 138 also make this mistake. Ten Berge 172-9 discusses at length *bouleusis* of unintentional homicide with special reference to Ant.6, and reaches a conclusion similar to mine.)

The case of Leon of Salamis is another which illustrates the meaning of *bouleusis*. In 404/3 the Thirty ordered five men, including Sokrates and Meletos (an accuser of Andokides in 400 or 399, to be distinguished from the Meletos who was an accuser of Sokrates in 399), to arrest Leon ; Sokrates refused, but the other four carried out the arrest, and the Thirty had Leon executed (And.1.94, Pl.*Ap*.32c-d, *Ep*.7.324e-325a). In 400 or 399 Andokides says that it would have been possible for the sons of Leon to prosecute Meletos for homicide, but for a recent law ordaining that prosecutions might not now be brought for offences committed before the year 403/2. And he quotes a law, showing that the charge which he claims could, but for the amnesty, have been brought against Meletos is one of *bouleusis*.

And.1.94. τὸν βουλεύσαντα ἐν τῷ αὐτῷ ἐνέχεσθαι καὶ τὸν τῇ χειρὶ ἐργασάμενον. ' A person who has planned is to be liable to the same treatment as one who has committed with his own hand.'

But this law raises a difficulty. Lipsius 125, followed by others, takes it to mean that the whole procedure in a case of *bouleusis* of intentional homicide was the same as in a case of intentional homicide committed with one's own hand, and therefore that cases of *bouleusis* of intentional homicide were tried on the Areopagos, not at the Palladion. I think that Lipsius is probably wrong, but it is necessary to review the various pieces of evidence individually.

1. *IG* i² 115.11-13 (quoted on page 118) lays down that cases of *bouleusis* are to be decided by the ephetai. But the context makes it almost certain that the reference here is to *bouleusis* of unintentional homicide, and the inscription says nothing about *bouleusis* of intentional homicide.

2. *Ath.Pol.*57.3 (quoted on page 58) states that cases of *bouleusis* are tried at the Palladion. Lipsius explains this passage by saying that the law must have been changed between the time of our extant fourth-century speeches in which the subject is mentioned and the date when the *Ath.Pol.* was written. But there is no other evidence for such a change. A different line is taken by Wilamowitz (*Aristoteles und Athen* i 252 note 138). He suggests that in this sentence the reference is to *bouleusis* of unintentional homicide only, ' of unintentional homicide ' being understood from the context ; it was necessary, he thinks, to say explicitly that there could be cases of *bouleusis* of unintentional homicide, whereas it could be taken for granted that cases of *bouleusis* of intentional homicide would be tried in the same court as cases of intentional homicide committed with one's own hand. Wilamowitz's arguments are not compelling. The logic of the sentence by no means demands that ' of unintentional homicide ' be understood with ' *bouleusis* ', since it is certainly not to be understood with the words that follow ; no one disputes that cases of the killing of slaves, metics, and foreigners were tried at the Palladion whether the homicide was alleged to be intentional or not.

And since ' planning ' homicide might be regarded as less serious than committing it with one's own hand, it is not really likely that the author of the *Ath.Pol.* would think it unnecessary to mention *bouleusis* of intentional homicide and say which court tried it, when he does think it necessary to say which court tried *bouleusis* of unintentional homicide. So probably Wilamowitz is wrong, and the *Ath.Pol.*'s statement may be taken as evidence that *bouleusis* of intentional as well as of unintentional homicide was tried at the Palladion. Nevertheless, it is just possible that Wilamowitz's interpretation is right ; and consequently this sentence of the *Ath.Pol.* is not by itself quite conclusive proof.

3. The law in And.1.94 (quoted on page 64) lays down that a person guilty of *bouleusis* is liable to the same treatment as one who has committed the offence with his own hand. This clearly means that he is liable to the same penalty. But does it mean that he is to be tried by the same court ? I do not think it necessarily means this ; consequently I do not think that this law is decisive in favour of Lipsius's view.

4. Antiphon 1 (*Against the Stepmother*), delivered in a case of *bouleusis* of intentional homicide, contains no indication of the court which heard it. At one point the speaker calls the jury ' helpers of those who are deliberately killed ' (Ant.1.22), but to say (as does Gernet *Antiphon* 34) that this expression can be applied only to the Areopagites is to beg the question whether cases of *bouleusis* of intentional homicide were not tried at the Palladion.

5. Lipsius 126-7 adduces Lysias 10 (the first speech *Against Theomnestos*), delivered in 384/3. The speaker says that in 404/3, when he was aged thirteen, his father was put to death by the Thirty (Lys.10.4). Later, as soon as he had passed his *dokimasia* (presumably at the age of eighteen, in 399/8), ' I proceeded against the Thirty on the Areopagos '

(Lys.10.31). Now, by 399/8 most members of the Thirty were either dead or in exile, and any who remained in Athens will already have undergone *euthynai* and thus become immune from further prosecution for offences committed in 404/3, in accordance with the terms of the amnesty of 403 (And.1.90, *Ath.Pol.*39.6). But an exception from the amnesty was made for cases of homicide committed with one's own hand (*Ath.Pol.*39.5). When the speaker says ' I proceeded against the Thirty ', he presumably means that he prosecuted one or two members of the Thirty who were still in Athens in 399/8. If so, the charge must have been one of committing homicide with their own hands, and this passage does not prove that cases of *bouleusis* were tried on the Areopagos.

6. Lipsius 127 adduces also Lysias 26 (*Against Euandros*). Euandros has been selected by lot for appointment as basileus, and is undergoing his *dokimasia* before taking office. The speaker attacks the appointment on the ground that Euandros held office under the Thirty, has ' unclean hands ' (Lys.26.8), and deserves rather to be tried by the Areopagos himself (Lys.26.12). But there is no proof that the speaker has in mind a case of *bouleusis* when he mentions the Areopagos. He may mean that Euandros has committed homicide with his own hands. More probably, the passage about the Areopagos is mere rhetoric and should not be taken literally.

7. In D.54.25 we read of a case in which a man (' the father of the priestess from Brauron ') was expelled by the Areopagos because he urged another man to strike a blow at a victim who afterwards died. Lipsius 127 takes this to mean that the man was accused of *bouleusis* of intentional homicide, was tried (or was due to be tried) on the Areopagos, and went into exile voluntarily to avoid condemnation. But this cannot be right ; ' the council of the Areo-

pagos expelled him' (ἐξέβαλεν) cannot mean that he went into exile voluntarily. It is not likely (and Lipsius himself does not maintain) that the Areopagos imposed exile as a penalty for *bouleusis* of intentional homicide, since the normal penalty for this offence was death. Nor is it likely (and Lipsius too rejects this alternative, which was suggested by Philippi 47-8, following Westermann) that the man was an Areopagite and that he was merely deprived of his membership of the Areopagos, since that would not be very relevant to the case of Konon with which the speech is concerned. I see only one other alternative not open to objection. The man must have been found guilty of deliberate wounding. The Areopagos regularly imposed exile as the penalty for this offence (Lys.3.42, 3.47, 4.20). If this is right, the passage is not evidence that the Areopagos tried cases of *bouleusis* of intentional homicide.

8. According to Harp. βουλεύσεως, Isaios in his speech *Against Eukleides* says that cases of *bouleusis* of homicide are tried at the Palladion, Deinarkhos in his speech *Against Pistias* says that they are tried on the Areopagos, and Aristotle in the *Ath.Pol.* agrees with Isaios. We have the *Ath.Pol.*, and can check that Harpokration's statement about it is correct (*Ath.Pol.*57.3); the speeches *Against Eukleides* and *Against Pistias* are lost. I do not know the explanation of the reference to the Areopagos. Possibly Harpokration has misunderstood what Deinarkhos wrote, and he himself seems to admit that what he takes to be Deinarkhos's meaning is contradicted by other evidence.

This reference by Harpokration to Deinarkhos is the only explicit and positive evidence for the view that cases of *bouleusis* of intentional homicide were tried on the Areopagos; and it could hardly be weaker than it is without ceasing to exist altogether. I prefer to accept what appears to me to be the natural interpretation of *Ath.Pol.*57.3, and to conclude that such cases were almost certainly tried at the Palladion.

The other kind of case which was tried at the Palladion, according to *Ath.Pol.*57.3, is that in which a person was accused of killing a slave, a metic, or a foreigner. There is no hint here of a distinction between intentional and unintentional killing, and the implication is that even the deliberate killing of such a person was not considered important enough for trial by the Areopagos. Examples of trials of this sort at the Palladion are the case of the slave of Kallimakhos's brother-in-law (Isok.18.52-4) and the case of Stephanos's slave (D.59.9-10), both described in chapter V. The case of the trierarkhos's old nurse, recounted in chapter II, would have been tried at the Palladion if the trierarkhos had decided to take legal action (D.47.70).

The wives and daughters of Athenian citizens, and sons who were still minors, are not included in the list of persons for killing whom trials were always held at the Palladion. Evidently trials for the intentional killing of such persons, like those for the intentional killing of full citizens, were held on the Areopagos. The same presumably applied to the killing of Athenian citizens who were disfranchised (ἄτι-μοι) because of debts owed to the state or for other reasons (see And.1.73-9 for various possible reasons for disfranchisement), but there is no evidence about trials of this sort.

Considered together, the kinds of case tried at the Palladion may seem a miscellaneous collection. But the principle is simply that this court heard those cases of homicide which were considered less important. All the more trivial cases went to it; the most serious kind of case, in which a person was accused of killing an Athenian citizen deliberately and with his own hand, was never tried here, but always on the Areopagos, at the Delphinion, or in Phreatto.

VII

THE DELPHINION

THE Delphinion was a temple of the twin deities of Delphoi, Apollon Delphinios and Artemis Delphinia, said to have been founded by the legendary king Aigeus on his return to Athens from Delphoi (Polyd.8.119, *Lexeis Rhetorikai* in *Lex.Seg.*255.19-21 ; cf. Plu.*Thes.*12.6). It was situated in south-east Athens, near the Olympieion (Paus.1.19.1 ; cf. Walther Judeich *Topographie von Athen²* 387). As at the Palladion, homicide cases will have been heard outside the temple, not in it.

Demosthenes, using somewhat elevated language, says that this court is the most holy and awesome of all the homicide courts (D.23.74 : πάντων ἁγιώτατα τούτων ἔχει καὶ φρικωδέστατα) ; here are heard cases in which a man admits killing, but says he did it lawfully. In the *Ath.Pol.* a similar definition is given, and examples are added.

*Ath.Pol.*57.3. ἐὰν δ' ἀποκτεῖναι μέν τις ὁμολογῇ, φῇ δὲ κατὰ τοὺς νόμους, οἷον μοιχὸν λαβὼν ἢ ἐν πολέμῳ ἀγνοήσας ἢ ἐν ἄθλῳ ἀγωνιζόμενος, τούτῳ ἐπὶ Δελφινίῳ δικάζουσιν. 'If a man admits killing, but says that he did it in accordance with the laws, for example catching a paramour, or unknowingly in war, or competing in a contest, they try him at the Delphinion.'

Some scholars have thought that cases were tried at the Delphinion only when all parties were agreed that the homicide which had been committed was lawful, so that the proceedings there were simply a kind of ceremonial absolution of the killer. Bonner and Smith ii 171 call both the Delphinion and the prytaneion ' purely ceremonial courts ', and Jones 260 states that the Delphinion court could not inflict the death penalty. But this is incorrect. If a man believed that another had committed homicide lawfully, the right thing to do was not to take him to court but ' to let him alone ' (Pl.*Euthphr*.4b : ἐᾶν). A case went to the Delphinion when a person was accused of unlawful homicide (whether intentional or unintentional) and defended himself not by denying that he committed homicide but by saying that he committed it lawfully. In other words, this court decided disputes not about whether a person had killed another, but about the circumstances in which he had done it. This is fairly clearly implied in the passages I have already quoted, D.23.74 and *Ath.Pol*.57.3, with their contrast between ὁμολογῇ and φῇ (' admits . . . but says . . .'). But it is clearer still in Arist.*Pol*.1300b24-30. In this passage Aristotle distinguishes four kinds of homicide court, and there is no doubt that he has in mind the Areopagos, Palladion, Delphinion, and Phreatto courts, although only the court in Phreatto is actually named. The third kind of court tries ' such cases as are admitted, but whose justice is disputed ' (ὅσα ὁμολογεῖται μέν, ἀμφισβητεῖται δὲ περὶ τοῦ δικαίου). The word ἀμφισβητεῖται shows plainly that the Delphinion court tried cases in which there was some dispute, and so was not ' purely ceremonial '.

A good instance of the kind of case tried at the Delphinion is provided by Lysias 1 (*For the Killing of Eratosthenes*). This speech is written for delivery by a man named Euphiletos. He is accused of deliberately killing Eratosthenes ; ' I now have at stake myself, my property, and everything else ', he says at the end of his speech (Lys.1.50), which shows that

F

he is liable to be condemned to the normal penalties for intentional homicide. In his defence he claims that he caught Eratosthenes in adultery with his wife, and killed him, and that it was lawful for him to do so. He calls as witnesses persons who saw him kill Eratosthenes, and he quotes laws to prove that killing in such circumstances is lawful. In other words, he 'admits killing, but says that he did it in accordance with the laws' (*Ath.Pol.*57.3)—a typical Delphinion case. At one point he quotes a law from the Areopagos.

Lys.1.30. ἀνάγνωθι δέ μοι καὶ τοῦτον τὸν νόμον ἐκ τῆς στήλης τῆς ἐξ Ἀρείου πάγου. ΝΟΜΟΣ. ἀκούετε, ὦ ἄνδρες, ὅτι αὐτῷ τῷ δικαστηρίῳ τῷ ἐξ Ἀρείου πάγου, ᾧ καὶ πάτριόν ἐστι καὶ ἐφ' ἡμῶν ἀποδέδοται τοῦ φόνου τὰς δίκας δικάζειν, διαρρήδην εἴρηται τοῦτον μὴ καταγιγνώ-σκειν φόνου, ὃς ἂν ἐπὶ δάμαρτι τῇ ἑαυτοῦ μοιχὸν λαβὼν ταύτην τὴν τιμωρίαν ποιήσηται. 'Please read also this law from the stone on the Areopagos. (*The law is read.*) You hear, gentlemen, that the court of the Areopagos itself, to which the trying of cases of homicide tradition-ally belongs and has been assigned in our own time too, is expressly forbidden to find guilty of homicide a man who catches a paramour in intercourse with his wife and punishes him in this way.'

The manner in which Euphiletos refers to the court of the Areopagos in the third person is further evidence (if further evidence were needed) that the present case, although it concerns a man who (as he claims) has caught a paramour in intercourse with his wife and killed him, is not being tried on the Areopagos but at the Delphinion. To what kind of case tried on the Areopagos, then, could this law apply ? The answer must be, to a case in which the accused denied committing homicide at all. If a man was accused

of killing someone deliberately (and unlawfully) and defended himself by saying that he did not kill him, the case
would naturally go to the Areopagos ; but it was possible
(as Lys.1.30 shows) that the Areopagos might find that he
had committed lawful homicide. Allocation of a case to a
particular court depended not on the verdict reached by the
jury (how could it ?), but on the nature of the charge and
the defence offered. The criterion for allocation of a case
to the Delphinion was that the accused man (not the accuser
nor necessarily the jury) said that he had committed homicide lawfully.

In what circumstances was homicide lawful ? Some are
listed in a law which Demosthenes quotes in the speech
Against Aristokrates, one of the many laws which he says
Aristokrates's proposal contravenes.

> D.23.53. ἐάν τις ἀποκτείνῃ ἐν ἄθλοις ἄκων, ἢ ἐν ὁδῷ
> καθελών, ἢ ἐν πολέμῳ ἀγνοήσας, ἢ ἐπὶ δάμαρτι ἢ ἐπὶ
> μητρὶ ἢ ἐπ' ἀδελφῇ ἢ ἐπὶ θυγατρί, ἢ ἐπὶ παλλακῇ ἣν ἂν
> ἐπ' ἐλευθέροις παισὶν ἔχῃ, τούτων ἕνεκα μὴ φεύγειν κτείν-
> αντα. 'If a man kills another in an athletic contest un-
> intentionally, or catching him waylaying him, or in war
> without knowing him, or in intercourse with his wife or
> his mother or his sister or his daughter or any concubine
> whom he keeps for begetting free children, exile is not
> to be imposed for killing for these reasons.'

This passage, together with others from the same speech,
*Ath.Pol.*57.3 (quoted on page 70), and a few references
elsewhere to relevant laws, enables us to make a list of
circumstances in which homicide was legally permitted.

1. Homicide committed by accident or mistake was excused in certain situations.

(*a*) In an athletic contest, such as boxing or wrestling, a
man who accidentally killed his opponent was not liable to

punishment (D.23.53, *Ath.Pol.*57.3). The words ' his opponent ' do not appear in the text of the law as we have it,
but Demosthenes in his discussion of it takes for granted
that the opposing contestant is the only kind of victim to
whom the law applies (D.23.54). A notorious puzzle concerned the case of the javelin-thrower who accidentally hit
and killed a spectator : was the thrower guilty of homicide,
or was it the fault of the javelin, or were the organizers of
the contest to blame for allowing spectators to stand where
they might be hit ? Perikles and Protagoras discussed this
problem (Plu.*Per.*36.5), which shows that the killing of a
spectator was not specifically excused in Athenian law. A
similar problem is the core of the imaginary case in Antiphon
3 (*Second Tetralogy*) : at a javelin-practice a boy has run
across the line of fire and been killed ; is the youth who
threw the javelin which hit him guilty of unintentional
homicide, or did the boy unintentionally commit suicide by
running across at the wrong time ? This problem has
nothing to do with the law excusing the killing of an opponent (though some scholars have confused them). A passive bystander is obviously in a quite different situation
from one who voluntarily enters the contest and thus agrees
by implication to ' take what is coming to him '.

(*b*) In war, a man who killed another in ignorance, mis-
taking him for an enemy, was not liable to punishment
(D.23.53, *Ath.Pol.*57.3).

(*c*) If a patient died while under the care of a doctor, the
doctor was not liable to punishment.

> Ant.4c.5. εἰ δέ τοι καὶ ὑπὸ τοῦ ἰατροῦ ἀπέθανεν, ὡς
> οὐκ ἀπέθανεν, ὁ μὲν ἰατρὸς οὐ φονεὺς αὐτοῦ ἐστιν, ὁ γὰρ
> νόμος ἀπολύει αὐτόν. ' And even if his death *was* due to
> the doctor (as it was not), the doctor is not guilty of
> killing him, for the law absolves him.'

Antiphon's use of ὑπό here indicates that the doctor was still absolved even if he caused the patient's death by negligence.

2. In some situations it was permissible to commit homicide in defence of oneself or one's property.

Ais.1.91. τῶν λωποδυτῶν ἢ τῶν μοιχῶν ἢ τῶν ἀνδροφόνων . . . οἱ μὲν ἐπ' αὐτοφώρῳ ἁλόντες, ἐὰν μὲν ὁμολογῶσι, παραχρῆμα θανάτῳ ζημιοῦνται. 'Robbers or paramours or killers . . . who are caught in the act, if they admit it, are immediately punished by death.'

But Aiskhines is speaking only in general terms. Killing in defence of oneself or one's property was permitted only in certain circumstances.

(a) A man who was attacked by another and in the course of defending himself killed his assailant was not liable to punishment ; but to prove his case he had to show that the other had struck the first blow. In the imaginary case of Antiphon 4 (*Third Tetralogy*) one of the chief lines of defence is precisely this, and witnesses are called (Ant.4d.3) to testify that the dead man himself began the fight which resulted in his death. A real case in which self-defence may have been pleaded is the case of Euaion (D.21.71-5). Boiotos, while drunk, struck Euaion a blow, and Euaion retaliated with such vigour that he killed Boiotos. At the trial the question was (according to Demosthenes, at least, though he has a motive for exaggerating this aspect of the case) whether one blow was enough to justify so violent a reprisal ; nearly half the jurors thought it was, and Euaion was convicted by a majority of only one vote.

(b) A special type of self-defence was the parrying of a highwayman's attack. This seems to be what is meant by the phrase ἐν ὁδῷ καθελών in D.23.53. The expression occurs nowhere else except in Harpokration's entry under ὁδός ;

he quotes the phrase from Demosthenes, and says that ἐν ὁδῷ is equivalent to ἐν λόχῳ καὶ ἐνέδρᾳ, ' in ambush '. We may translate ἐν ὁδῷ ' waylaying '.

Lipsius 616 note 59 rejects this interpretation ; but he has here fallen below his usual standard of perspicacity. He first dismisses Harpokration's explanation out-of-hand as untenable, and then raises the possibility that ἐν ὁδῷ may refer to highwaymen, apparently without seeing that Harpokration's explanation may well refer to highwaymen. Next, following Bergk, he puts forward a grammatical objection : if ἐν ὁδῷ refers to highwaymen, it must qualify the object of καθελών, and yet no object is expressed. But a quite adequate parallel for this omission is provided by the later part of the same sentence, where ἐπὶ δάμαρτι . . . qualifies the unexpressed object. Lipsius does not suggest any alternative interpretation.

(c) It was permissible to kill a brigand in defence of one's property. But again certain conditions had to be fulfilled : only the owner of stolen property could exercise this right ; the robber had to be using force ; the killing had to be immediate, not after a lapse of time. This law too is quoted in the speech *Against Aristokrates*.

D.23.60. ἐὰν φέροντα ἢ ἄγοντα βίᾳ ἀδίκως εὐθὺς ἀμυνόμενος κτείνῃ, νηποινεὶ τεθνάναι. ' If one kills immediately in defence of one's property a man carrying or leading it away by force unjustly, he is to be killed with impunity.'

Demosthenes goes on to discuss the law, and stresses the significance of ' immediately ' and ' in defence of one's property ' (D.23.60-1).

(d) It was permissible to kill anyone caught stealing anything at night (D.24.113). This rule would apply to such persons as housebreakers who would not necessarily use force and so would not be covered by (c).

(*e*) An Athenian regarded the female members of his family as in some sense analogous to his property, and a man was permitted to kill a paramour caught in sexual intercourse with his wife, mother, sister, daughter, or ' any concubine whom he keeps for begetting free children ' (D.23.53; cf. Lys.1, Plu.*Sol*.23.1). The last item in this list would include a foreign-born wife. An Athenian could not legally marry a woman who was not of Athenian parentage on both sides. Such a wife had to be regarded legally as a concubine, though in other respects she might well be treated in the same way as an Athenian wife.

It has been thought (by Philippi 56) that a similar law permitted the killing by a boy's father or brother of a man caught in a homosexual act with him. But this is disproved by Lys.1.32, where the lawfulness of killing a woman's paramour is made a point of contrast between the punishments assigned to heterosexual and to homosexual offences.

3. It was permissible to kill persons who committed certain kinds of offence against the state.

(*a*) If a man who had been sentenced to exile for homicide was found within Athenian territory, he might be killed with impunity (*IG* i² 115.30-1, D.23.28).

(*b*) It was lawful (at least at certain periods) to kill anyone who attempted to set up a tyranny or overthrow the democracy. There is first an early law quoted in the *Ath.Pol.*

> *Ath.Pol.*16.10. ἐάν τινες τυραννεῖν ἐπανιστῶνται [ἐπὶ τυραννίδι], ἢ συγκαθιστῇ τὴν τυραννίδα, ἄτιμον εἶναι καὶ αὐτὸν καὶ γένος. ' Any who set themselves up to be tyrants, or is [*sic*] associated in the establishment of the tyranny, is to be outlawed, both himself and his family.'

It is generally agreed (see the references given by Ostwald in *TAPA* lxxxvi 107 note 18) that ἄτιμον here means ' outlawed'; this implies that the offender might be killed with impunity. The author of the *Ath.Pol.* refers the law vaguely to the time of Peisistratos, but we have no definite information about the date at which it was made or the date at which it ceased to be valid.

Next comes the decree of Demophantos. I quote part of it only.

And.1.96. ἐάν τις δημοκρατίαν καταλύῃ τὴν ᾿Αθήνησιν, ἢ ἀρχήν τινα ἄρχῃ καταλελυμένης τῆς δημοκρατίας, πολέμιος ἔστω ᾿Αθηναίων καὶ νηποινεὶ τεθνάτω, καὶ τὰ χρήματα αὐτοῦ δημόσια ἔστω, καὶ τῆς θεοῦ τὸ ἐπιδέκατον· ὁ δὲ ἀποκτείνας τὸν ταῦτα ποιήσαντα καὶ ὁ συμβουλεύσας ὅσιος ἔστω καὶ εὐαγής. 'If anyone overthrows the democracy at Athens, or holds any office when the democracy has been overthrown, he shall be an enemy of the Athenians and shall be killed with impunity, and his property shall be confiscated and a tenth part of it devoted to the Goddess ; and he who kills or helps to plan the killing of such a man shall be pure and free from guilt.'

This decree was passed in 410. Ostwald (*TAPA* lxxxvi 115-19) maintains that it was superseded in or soon after 403 by the law on impeachment (νόμος εἰσαγγελτικός) which is quoted by Hyp.4.7-8. However, he is mistaken in concluding from And.1.99 that the decree did not survive the legal reforms of 403. (The law quoted there, 'the laws must be enforced from the arkhonship of Eukleides', does not mean ' no law passed before 403/2 is valid ', but ' no one is to be prosecuted for an offence against the laws which was committed before 403/2 '. Cf. my *Andokides : On the Mysteries* 128-9.) D.20.159 and Lyk.124-7 show that the stone on which the decree of Demophantos was inscribed remained in place in the fourth century, and this implies that the decree was not formally annulled (though it may have fallen into disuse). Ostwald seems to assume that the decree of Demophantos and the law on impeachment could not have coexisted ; but it is more likely that anyone who caught a traitor to the democracy was allowed either to kill him out-of-hand or to impeach him, whichever he preferred.

Thirdly there is the law of Eukrates (preserved in an inscription published by B. D. Meritt in *Hesperia* xxi [1952] 355-6). Part of it runs thus.

SEG xii 87.7-11.

ἐάν τις ἐπαναστῆι τῶι δήμωι ἐπὶ τυραννίδι
ἢ τὴν τυραννίδα συνκαταστήσηι ἢ τὸν δῆμον τ-
ὸν Ἀθηναίων ἢ τὴν δημοκρατίαν τὴν Ἀθήνησιν
καταλύσηι, ὃς ἂν τὸν τούτων τι ποιήσαντα ἀπο-
κτείνηι ὅσιος ἔστω.

' If anyone sets himself up against the people with a view to tyranny, or is associated in the establishment of the tyranny, or overthrows the people of Athens or the democracy at Athens, whoever kills the man who does any of these things shall be free from guilt.'

From its wording it is clear that this law is based on the two earlier ones. It was passed in 336, but was perhaps repealed before 331/0 (as Ostwald argues in *TAPA* lxxxvi 127-8).

This completes, as far as our evidence goes, the list of circumstances in which homicide was lawful. The range of situations was wide, at least by modern standards. Under modern legal codes the killing of a nocturnal thief or an adulterer, for example, would not be condoned ; but in Athens in the fifth and fourth centuries there was a much more recent tradition of self-help. It seemed natural that a man who stole one's property or one's wife should be resisted by an immediate use of force, instead of being calmly referred to some higher authority for trial, and there had probably never been a period when killing in such circumstances was not permitted. The usual direction of development for a society is from habits of self-help towards the use of legal trials ; so the fact that an Athenian was still permitted in the fourth century to kill a nocturnal thief or an adulterer for himself instead of taking him to court shows that Athenian society in this respect remained primitive.

It is in this light that we may understand the law which ordered Athenians ' to kill neither justly nor unjustly ' (μήτε δικαίως μήτε ἀδίκως ἀποκτείνειν) which is mentioned four times in the *Tetralogies* attributed to Antiphon (Ant.3b.9, 3c.7, 4b.3, 4d.8). Some have denied this to be a genuine Athenian law, on the ground that the known laws about various kinds of lawful homicide, and indeed the very existence of the court at the Delphinion, prove that there cannot have been a law forbidding Athenians to kill justly ; and W. Dittenberger (in *Hermes* xxxi [1896] 271-7, xxxii [1897] 1-41, xl [1905] 450-70) used this law as one of the main props for his argument that the *Tetralogies* were not written by Antiphon or by an Athenian author at all. I do not wish to discuss here whether Antiphon wrote the *Tetralogies*. But I am satisfied that, whoever their author, their legal background is Athenian (cf. Maidment 46, and also my remarks on the *Second* and *Third Tetralogies* on pages 74-5), that if the law forbidding just killing had not existed the author would not have said that it did, and that it may therefore be accepted as an Athenian law. A careful distinction must be made between just killing and lawful killing (cf. Maschke 53 note 1). The court at the Delphinion acquitted persons who had killed lawfully (D.23.74 ἐννόμως, *Ath.Pol.*57.3 κατὰ τοὺς νόμους ; cf. the stress laid on the laws throughout Lys.1). But some kinds of killing were just but not lawful. For example, if a man's father was killed it might be just for him to kill the killer, but it was not lawful, since the law prescribed a procedure for prosecuting killers. So the law forbidding just as well as unjust killing means that, even if a man deserves to be killed, one may not kill him (except in the particular circumstances, specified in other laws, in which killing is lawful) but must proceed against him by legal methods. This law (as Paoli rightly maintains in *RIDA* I i 158-60, though I disagree with some details of his argument) marks a stage in the process of development from self-help to reliance on legal action. Thus the laws limiting the circumstances in which homicide by an aggrieved person was permitted, and the Delphinion court which examined claims that particular killings were lawful, may be regarded as symbols of progress, not of primitiveness.

VIII

IN PHREATTO

ANOTHER homicide court was the one sometimes called ' in Phreatto '. Both the name and the location are doubtful.

The two commonest forms of the name are ἐν Φρεαττοῖ, which implies a nominative Φρεαττώ (or possibly Φρεαττώς), ' in Phreatto ', and ἐν Φρεάτου, ' in the sanctuary of Phreatos '. But other forms also occur : the τ may or may not be doubled, giving ἐν Φρεατοῖ or ἐν Φρεάττου, and Pausanias, the only writer to use the word in the nominative, gives Φρεαττύς. The evidence is as follows. In D.23.77-8 most manuscripts have ἐν Φρεαττοῖ, but S, the most important of them, according to the *apparatus criticus* of Sykutris in the Teubner edition, has ἐν Φρεαττου (without accent). In Arist. *Pol.*1300b29 one manuscript has ἐν Φρεατοῖ, the others ἐν Φρεαττοῖ. *Ath.Pol.*57.3 has ἐν Φρεάτου. Paus.1.28.11 has Φρεαττύς. The manuscripts of Harpokration, in his article on the phrase, are divided between ἐν Φρεατοῖ and ἐν Φρεάτου. Harpokration gives Theophrastos *Laws* as his authority for saying that the court was named after a hero Phreatos, and this shows that the form ἐν Φρεάτου (or ἐν Φρεάττου) is at least as old as Theophrastos ; but it does not prove that form to be better than ἐν Φρεαττοῖ (or ἐν Φρεατοῖ), for which Theophrastos may have been attempting to find an etymological explanation. In Harpokration's article on ἐφέται, the manuscripts offer ἐν Φρεάτοις. Other late writers have ἐν (or ἐμ) Φρεαττοῖ or Φρεατοῖ, with some variations of accent (Polyd.8.120, schol. on Ar.*Pl.*1166, *Lexeis Rhetorikai*

82

in *Lex.Seg.*311.20, Souda ἐμ Φρεάτοι). From this evidence no definite conclusion can be drawn. When I use the expression ' in Phreatto ', I am not confident that this name is correct.

Most of the authors who mention the court say that it was beside the sea ; Paus.1.28.11 adds that it was at Peiraieus ; but no one gives exact evidence about its location. But in *Lexeis Rhetorikai* two similar courts are mentioned.

> *Lexeis Rhetorikai* in *Lex.Seg.*311.17-22. ἐν Ζέᾳ· τόπος ἐστὶ παράλιος. ἐνταῦθα κρίνεται ὁ ἐπ᾽ ἀκουσίῳ μὲν φόνῳ φεύγων, αἰτίαν δὲ ἔχων ἐπὶ ἑκουσίῳ φόνῳ.
>
> ἐν Φρεαττοῖ· οἱ ἐπ᾽ ἀκουσίῳ φόνῳ φεύγοντες, ἐπ᾽ ἄλλῳ δέ τινι κρινόμενοι· οἳ ἐπὶ πλοίῳ ἑστῶτες ἀπολογοῦνται.

There is no other evidence of a court in Zea, and the two descriptions here are so alike that it seems probable that the courts in Zea and in Phreatto were one and the same, wrongly assumed by the lexicographer to be distinct. If so, Phreatto was at Zea, on the east side of Peiraieus. (This is the view of Walther Judeich *Topographie von Athen*[2] 436.)

Demosthenes quotes a law stating the kind of offender tried at this court.

> D.23.77. ἐάν τις ἐπ᾽ ἀκουσίῳ φόνῳ πεφευγώς, μήπω τῶν ἐκβαλλόντων αὐτὸν ᾐδεσμένων, αἰτίαν ἔχῃ ἑτέρου φόνου ἑκουσίου. ' Anyone who, after being exiled for unintentional homicide, when his banishers have not yet pardoned him, is accused of committing another homicide intentionally.'

The second homicide presumably might be one which the accused man had committed before he was banished for the first, or it might be one which he committed while in exile, by killing an Athenian outside Attica. The court sat on the beach ; the accused arrived by boat, and made his defence from the boat, ' casting neither gangway nor anchor on to the land ' (Polyd.8.120), so that he did not infringe his exile by touching Attic ground (D.23.78). Why would an accused man already in exile be willing to return for a trial at which he might be condemned to death ? Presumably because unless he secured an acquittal on the charge of intentional homicide he would not be able to return to Attica when he eventually obtained pardon (αἴδεσις ; see chapter XII) for his unintentional homicide. Whether an accused man not willing to face trial might be extradited from foreign territory for a trial in Phreatto is not known.

Aristotle (Pol.1300b29-30) plausibly says that ' few such cases ever occur, even in large cities '. (Miles, in RIDA I v 219-24, therefore postulates some other kinds of trial to help occupy the court's time. But his account is based partly on a mistranslation of ἐπὶ καθόδῳ in Arist.Pol.1300b28, which means not ' on their return ' but ' with a view to their return ', partly on a misinterpretation of the law in D.23.82, which I discuss on pages 27-31, and partly on conjecture unsupported by evidence.) There is no recorded instance of a trial in Phreatto ; and Aristotle's words οἷον Ἀθήνησι λέγεται καὶ τὸ ἐν Φρεαττοῖ δικαστήριον, ' such as at Athens the court in Phreatto is said to be ', seem to imply that he had never known the court to sit.

IX

THE PRYTANEION AND THE PHYLOBASILEIS

THE prytaneion was a building on the northern side of the akropolis. It was used for various official purposes, and among them as a law-court. We have several accounts of the kind of case tried there.

D.23.76. ἐὰν λίθος ἢ ξύλον ἢ σίδηρος ἤ τι τοιοῦτον ἐμπεσὸν πατάξῃ, καὶ τὸν μὲν βαλόντ' ἀγνοῇ τις, αὐτὸ δ' εἰδῇ καὶ ἔχῃ τὸ τὸν φόνον εἰργασμένον, τούτοις ἐνταῦθα λαγχάνεται. ' If a piece of stone or wood or iron or anything of that sort falls on a person and hits him, and one is ignorant of the thrower but knows and has the actual object which accomplished the homicide, one brings a case there against these.'

Patmos schol. on D.23.76 (published in *Bulletin de Correspondance Hellénique* i [1877] 139). ἐπὶ πρυτανείῳ· ἐν τούτῳ τῷ δικαστηρίῳ δικάζονται φόνου, ὅταν ὁ μὲν ἀνῃρημένος δῆλος ᾖ, ζητεῖται [ζητῆται Wilamowitz] δὲ ὁ τὸν φόνον δράσας. καὶ ἀποφέρει τὴν γραφὴν πρὸς τὸν βασιλέα, καὶ ὁ βασιλεὺς διὰ τοῦ κήρυκος κηρύττει καὶ ἀπαγορεύει τόνδε τὸν ἀνελόντα τὸν δεῖνα μὴ ἐπιβαίνειν ἱερῶν καὶ χώρας Ἀττικῆς. ἐν τῷ αὐτῷ δὲ τούτῳ δικαστηρίῳ κἄν τι ἐμπεσὸν πατάξῃ τινὰ καὶ ἀνέλῃ τῶν ἀψύχων, δικάζεται τούτῳ καὶ ὑπερορίζεται. ' At the prytaneion : in this court they are tried for homicide whenever a person is known to have been killed but the person who committed the homicide is missing. One delivers the written accusation to the

85

basileus, and the basileus makes an announcement through the herald and forbids this man who killed so-and-so to set foot in holy places and the land of Attica. Also, if an inanimate object falling on someone hits him and kills him, a trial is held for it in this same court and it is cast beyond the frontier.'

Polyd. 8.120. τὸ ἐπὶ πρυτανείῳ δικάζει περὶ τῶν ἀπο-κτεινάντων, κἂν ὦσιν ἀφανεῖς, δικάζει δὲ καὶ περὶ τῶν ἀψύχων τῶν ἐμπεσόντων καὶ ἀποκτεινάντων. προειστήκε-σαν δὲ τούτου τοῦ δικαστηρίου οἱ φυλοβασιλεῖς, οὓς ἔδει τὸ ἐμπεσὸν ἄψυχον ὑπερορίσαι. ' The court at the prytaneion tries cases about killers even if they are unknown, and also cases about inanimate objects which have fallen on some-one and killed him. The phylobasileis were in charge of this court, and it was their duty to cast beyond the frontier the object which had fallen on someone.'

In the final sentences of *Ath.Pol.*57 the reference is evidently to the prytaneion, although it is not mentioned by name.

*Ath.Pol.*57.4. ὅταν δὲ μὴ εἰδῇ τὸν ποιήσαντα, τῷ δρά-σαντι λαγχάνει. δικάζει δ' ὁ βασιλεὺς καὶ οἱ φυλοβασιλεῖς καὶ τὰς τῶν ἀψύχων καὶ τῶν ἄλλων ζῴων. 'When one does not know who did it, one brings a case against " the doer ". The basileus and the phylobasileis try also the cases of inanimate objects and of animals besides.'

By fitting these pieces of evidence together we can get some idea of the activities of the court. Although Demosthenes mentions only charges against inanimate objects, it is clear from the other passages that the court also heard cases against animals, and cases against unknown human killers even when no inanimate instrument was found—in short, any case in which a man was killed and his relatives could find no individual human being to accuse. This would cover a man who happened to be walking under a tree when it blew down on top of him, a man gored by a bull, or a man killed by a stone thrown by an unseen hand, whether the stone was found or not.

Polydeukes says that the phylobasileis were in charge; but the *Ath.Pol.* shows that they acted with the basileus, and Polydeukes himself elsewhere (8.90) says that the basileus tried cases of inanimate objects, and so his omission of the basileus in 8.120 must be merely a slip. The phylobasileis were the heads of the four ancient Athenian tribes. These four tribes were superseded for political purposes by the ten tribes instituted by Kleisthenes in 508/7, but they retained some religious functions. So in the fifth and fourth centuries the duties of the phylobasileis were mainly religious (Polyd.8.111).

There is some doubt whether they took part in the proceedings in other homicide courts besides the prytaneion. In the sentence in the *Ath.Pol.*, ' the basileus and the phylobasileis try also the cases of inanimate objects . . .', it is possible that the word ' also ' implies ' as well as all other homicide cases '. In the law about unintentional homicide (*IG* i² 115.12), in Solon's amnesty law (Plu.*Sol.*19.4), and in the decree of Patrokleides (And.1.78), persons accused of homicide are said to be tried by ' the basileis ', in the plural. This may mean the basileus and the phylobasileis, and may imply that the phylobasileis were associated with the basileus in all the homicide courts. But all these passages can be interpreted otherwise. In the *Ath.Pol.* ' also ' may imply merely ' as well as cases of unknown killers '. And the plural ' basileis ' in the other passages may mean ' the basileus of each individual year '. I do not know which alternative is right. In favour of the view that the prytaneion

G

court was the only one in which the phylobasileis partici-
pated, one might argue that otherwise the author of the
Ath.Pol. would have mentioned them earlier in his account
of the homicide courts, and not merely in the last sentence.
But this is not a strong argument, and it remains possible
that they accompanied the basileus in other homicide courts
besides the prytaneion.

Was there a jury in this court ? Both Harpokration and
Polydeukes include it in the list of courts in which cases
were tried by the ephetai (Harp. ἐφέται, Polyd.8.125, both
quoted on pages 48-9). But in Arist.*Pol.*1300b24-30 and *Ath.
Pol.*57.3-4, when lists are given of the four kinds of homicide
courts in which juries sat, the prytaneion appears to be
deliberately excluded. And Solon's amnesty law (Plu.*Sol.*
19.4) refers to persons condemned by the Areopagos or the
ephetai or the prytaneion (ὅσοι ἐξ 'Αρείου πάγου ἢ ὅσοι ἐκ
τῶν ἐφετῶν ἢ ἐκ πρυτανείου καταδικασθέντες . . . ἔφευγον),
which may possibly imply that these three alternatives were
mutually exclusive. So perhaps Harpokration and Polydeukes (or some predecessor whom both copied) made a
mistake in including it among the ephetai's courts.

An object found to have killed a person was cast beyond
the frontiers of Attica by the phylobasileis (Ais.3.244, Paus.
6.11.6, Polyd.8.120, Patmos schol. on D.23.76). What happened to an animal found to have killed a person is not
known. Plato (*Laws* 873e) orders such animals to be killed
and cast beyond the frontiers, and Düll (*ZSSR* lxi 7-10)
concludes that this was the rule in Athens, but here as elsewhere Plato's law may differ from Athenian law. When an
unknown person was accused as ' the doer ' (*Ath.Pol.*57.4),
the court pronounced against him and the basileus declared
him an exile ; this is shown not only by the statement of the
Patmos schaliast but also by passages in the amnesty laws

(And.1.78, Plu.*Sol.*19.4) which refer to persons condemned at the prytaneion.

The existence and procedure of this court are an outstanding example of the operation of ritual in Athenian homicide law.   Yet it is not on that account to be regarded as entirely absurd and pointless.   If someone was killed by an object, an animal, or an unknown person, it was desirable that the state should take note of the manner of his death, and take any steps that were practicable to see that no one else died in the same way in future.   The court served some of the purposes of a modern coroner's court.

X

OATHS

THE five courts which I have now described (Areopagos, Palladion, Delphinion, Phreatto, prytaneion) were the ones which were particularly concerned with homicide. I shall call them 'the special homicide courts', though this phrase must not be taken to imply that they tried only homicide cases (for the Areopagos, at least, heard other kinds of case too), nor that they were the only courts which could try homicide cases. It was also possible to bring a killer before an ordinary heliastic court by the procedure called *apagoge*, which I shall describe in chapter XIII. But before I go on to *apagoge*, I shall first discuss some features of procedure which were common to all or some of the special homicide courts.

Antiphon draws attention to the fact that the procedure in a trial for homicide differed from that in other kinds of trial.

Ant.6.6. οἵ τε νόμοι καὶ αἱ διωμοσίαι καὶ τὰ τόμια καὶ αἱ προρρήσεις, καὶ τἆλλα ὅσα γίγνεται τῶν δικῶν τοῦ φόνου ἕνεκα, πολὺ διαφέροντά ἐστιν ἢ ἐπὶ τοῖς ἄλλοις. 'The laws, the oaths, the cut pieces, the proclamations, and all the other things that are done for homicide trials are very different from what is done for other cases.'

Demosthenes gives a more detailed account of the oaths and the 'cut pieces'.

D.23.67-8. ἐν Ἀρείῳ πάγῳ, οὗ δίδωσ' ὁ νόμος καὶ

κελεύει τοῦ φόνου δικάζεσθαι, πρῶτον μὲν διομεῖται κατ'
ἐξωλείας αὐτοῦ καὶ γένους καὶ οἰκίας ὅ τιν' αἰτιώμενος
εἰργάσθαι τι τοιοῦτον, εἶτ' οὐδὲ τὸν τυχόντα τιν' ὅρκον
[τοῦτο ποιήσει] ἀλλ' ὃν οὐδεὶς ὄμνυσ' ὑπὲρ οὐδενὸς ἄλλου,
στὰς ἐπὶ τῶν τομίων κάπρου καὶ κριοῦ καὶ ταύρου, καὶ
τούτων ἐσφαγμένων ὑφ' ὧν δεῖ καὶ ἐν αἷς ἡμέραις καθήκει,
ὥστε καὶ ἐκ τοῦ χρόνου καὶ ἐκ τῶν μεταχειριζομένων ἄπαν,
ὅσον ἔσθ' ὅσιον, πεπρᾶχθαι. καὶ μετὰ ταῦθ' ὁ τὸν τοιοῦτον
ὅρκον ὀμωμοκὼς οὔπω πεπίστευται, ἀλλ' ἐὰν ἐξελεγχθῇ
μὴ λέγων ἀληθῆ, τὴν ἐπιορκίαν ἀπενεγκάμενος τοῖς αὐτοῦ
παισὶν καὶ τῷ γένει πλέον οὐδ' ὁτιοῦν ἕξει. ' On the Areopagos, where the law allows and orders trials for homicide
to be held, first the man who accuses someone of such a
deed will swear an oath invoking destruction on himself
and his family and his house, and no ordinary oath either,
but one which no one swears on any other subject, standing over the cut pieces of a boar, a ram, and a bull, which
have been slaughtered by the right persons and on the
proper days, so that every religious requirement has been
fulfilled both as regards the time and as regards the execu-
tants. And after this the man who has sworn this solemn
oath is not trusted even then, but if he is proved to be
lying he will bring perjury home to his children and his
family and will not gain anything by it at all.'

The ' cut pieces ' are mentioned also in a passage in which
Aiskhines describes an oath taken at the end of the trial by
the winner.

Ais.2.87.   πῶς οὐκ εἰκότως οἱ πατέρες ἡμῶν ἐν ταῖς
φονικαῖς δίκαις ἐπὶ Παλλαδίῳ κατέδειξαν τέμνοντας τὰ
τόμια τοὺς νικῶντας τῇ ψήφῳ ἐξορκίζεσθαι, καὶ τοῦτο ὑμῖν
πάτριόν ἐστιν ἔτι καὶ νῦν, τἀληθῆ καὶ τὰ δίκαια ψηφίζεσθαι
τῶν δικαστῶν ὅσοι τὴν ψῆφον ἤνεγκαν αὐτῷ, καὶ ψεῦδος
μηδὲν εἰρηκέναι, εἰ δὲ μή, ἐξώλη τ' αὐτὸν εἶναι ἐπαρᾶσθαι
καὶ τὴν οἰκίαν τὴν αὑτοῦ, τοῖς δὲ δικασταῖς εὔχεσθαι πολλὰ

καὶ ἀγαθὰ εἶναι; 'In homicide trials at the Palladion our ancestors very properly introduced the rule (and you have retained this tradition up to the present day) that those who are victorious in the voting cut the cut pieces and swear that those of the jurors who voted for him were making the true and right decision, and that he has spoken no lie, and that otherwise he invokes destruction on himself and his house, but prays that the jurors may have many blessings.'

Oaths in which the swearer invoked destruction on himself and his house if his statements were false were used on other occasions besides homicide trials (e.g. *IG* i² 10.15-16, And.1.98, 126, Lys.12.10, D.24.151); this form of words was a common one for a solemn oath. And although the oath at homicide trials was called *diomosia*, the term διόμνυσθαι was used also of oaths taken on other occasions (e.g. Is.11.6, Ais.3.149, D.18.283). The thing that was peculiar to homicide trials was the external circumstances in which the oath was taken: a particular sacrificial ritual had to be performed. An 'oath-administerer' (ὁρκωτής) is mentioned in one passage (Ant.6.14); he doubtless supervised the ritual.

The accuser swore that his accusation was true and that the accused had committed the homicide (Ant.6.16, Lys. 10.11, D.23.67, 59.10). The accused swore that his defence was true and that he had not committed the homicide (Ant. 6.16, Lys.10.11, D.23.69). At least, this is what they swore on the Areopagos and at the Palladion. Obviously at the Delphinion the accused will not have sworn that he did not commit the homicide, and at the prytaneion the accused (being either unknown or an animal or an inanimate object) will not have sworn at all; but we have no further information about the oaths at these two courts and in Phreatto.

(A.*Eu*.429, referred to by Bonner and Smith ii 170, is spoken on the akropolis, and so proves nothing about the court at the Delphinion.) The winner, but not the loser, swore to the truth of his case again after the verdict (Ais.2.87). In the text of Aiskhines, this oath after the verdict is connected with the Palladion court only; but the words ἐπὶ Παλλαδίῳ have sometimes been deleted as a gloss (cf. Philippi in *Rheinisches Museum* xxix [1874] 10-11), and whether they are a gloss or not one would expect that the practice would be the same in the other special homicide courts.

At the beginning of the trial the accuser and accused swore also to make their speeches relevant to the charge. In Antiphon 5 the man accused of killing Herodes describes what would have happened if his opponent had (as he actually has not) brought a normal charge of homicide against him.

Ant.5.11. τοῦτο δὲ δέον σε διομόσασθαι ὅρκον τὸν μέγιστον καὶ ἰσχυρότατον, ἐξώλειαν σαυτῷ καὶ γένει καὶ οἰκίᾳ τῇ σῇ ἐπαρώμενον, ἦ μὴν μὴ ἄλλα κατηγορήσειν ἐμοῦ ἢ εἰς αὐτὸν τὸν φόνον, ὡς ἔκτεινα, . . . 'And secondly, because you ought to have sworn the greatest and mightiest oath, invoking destruction on yourself, your family, and your house, that you would not bring any other accusations against me except for the actual homicide, that I killed him, . . .'

The khoregos mentions a law that an accuser must keep to the point (Ant.6.9 : εἰς αὐτὸ τὸ πρᾶγμα κατηγορεῖν), and the Areopagos had its own rule about irrelevance (see pages 43-4) ; we know too that an oath to keep to the point was sworn by both parties in *dikai* in heliastic courts (*Ath.Pol.* 67.1). Thus it need not be doubted (as it is by Mederle 16, Glotz *Études sociales* 151-2) that irrelevance was mentioned in the oath at homicide trials.

Did the accuser include in his oath a declaration that he was entitled to prosecute because he was a relative of the killed person (or the master of a killed slave) ? The view that he did is taken by Philippi 80, Mederle 17, Lipsius 831, Bonner and Smith ii 166. The only evidence for it comes from the case of the trierarkhos and the old nurse (D.47.68-73, quoted on pages 13-14). Three sentences are relevant to this problem.

(*a*) ' " It is not legally your concern, since, from what you say, the woman is not a relative or slave of yours, and it is for these that the laws order prosecution to be undertaken ; so that if you yourself and your wife and children take the oath at the Palladion and invoke destruction on yourselves and your house, many will think you ignoble, and if he is acquitted you will be thought to have committed perjury, and if he is convicted you will be unpopular." '

My interpretation of this sentence is as follows. The law said that relatives (or the master of a slave) were required to prosecute for homicide. It said nothing about whether others might prosecute. (Cf. my discussion of this point on pages 17-18.) If the trierarkhos prosecuted Theophemos for homicide when not legally required to, people would think that he was motivated only by enmity towards Theophemos. They would regard him as a malicious accuser (συκοφάντης), whether he won his case or not. If he did not win it, they would also think that he had lied when he swore that Theophemos killed the nurse.

Those who believe that the law positively forbade anyone to prosecute for homicide except relatives (or the master of a slave), and that a prosecutor had to swear that he was a relative (or master) of the killed person, have to offer a different interpretation, something like this. If the trier-

arkhos prosecuted, he would swear a false oath that the
nurse was his relative or slave. If it was discovered that
his oath was false, Theophemos would be acquitted, and
the trierarkhos would be thought a perjurer. If his oath
was believed, and Theophemos was convicted,—why would
he be unpopular ? This is the point where this interpretation runs into difficulty. It is plainly stated in the text that
unpopularity and a reputation for ignoble conduct would
be the result (ὥστ’) of the law that one must prosecute for
the homicide of a relative or slave. This must mean that
the trierarkhos would be unpopular if people knew that he
was prosecuting for a person not his relative or slave. Yet
even so he could still win his case. This proves that it was
legally possible to prosecute for the homicide of a person
who was not one's relative or slave, and consequently that
the prosecutor was not required to swear that the killed
person was his relative or slave.

(b) ' I should not have dared to lie to you and take the
oath for myself, my son, and my wife, not even if I were
sure of getting these men convicted ; for I do not hate
them as much as I love myself.'

According to my interpretation the trierarkhos, if he
prosecuted Theophemos and Euergos, had two alternative
ways of setting about it. He could acknowledge that the
nurse was not his relative or slave, and thus incur odium,
as I have just explained in my comments on sentence (a).
Alternatively he could claim, in the course of his prosecution, that she was a relative or slave. But this would mean
telling a lie to the jury ; and since he would have sworn in
his oath that he was speaking the truth in his prosecution,
he might have brought destruction on himself and his house.
I take καὶ to be adversative : ' to lie and yet also to take the

oath '. (Cf. J. D. Denniston *The Greek Particles*[2] 292.)

Those who think that the oath itself contained a declaration that the killed person was the accuser's relative or slave naturally take this phrase as a hendiadys : ' to swear a false oath '. Either of these interpretations is possible grammatically.

(*c*) ' The law orders the relatives to take proceedings, as far as sons of cousins (it also defines in the oath what constitutes a " relative ").' (Polyd.8.118, as I pointed out on page 16, is based on this passage and cannot be regarded as independent evidence.)

What oath ? The oath sworn by the accuser at the trial ? The speaker does not say so. In the surviving parts of *IG* i² 115, which was probably the ' law of Drakon ' which the trierarkhos consulted, the only oath mentioned is one which certain relatives (but not father, brother, or sons) swore when extending pardon to a man exiled for unintentional homicide. The oath containing a definition of ' relative ' may have been this one ; or it may have been some other. There is no way of telling for certain. But at any rate (*c*) is too vague to be used as evidence that the accuser's oath at the trial contained a declaration about his relationship to the dead person.

Of these three sentences, (*a*) is the decisive one, showing that the accuser did not have to swear that the killed person was his relative or slave.

Some have thought (Philippi 87, Lipsius 831, Bonner and Smith ii 167-9) that the oaths were sworn at the *prodikasiai*, either as well as or instead of being sworn at the trial. But their only ground for this view seems to be the belief that the accuser's oath contained a declaration of his relationship to the killed person and that the basileus would not have made arrangements for a trial until this declaration had been made. If I am right in my argument that the accuser was not required to make any such declaration, no reason remains for assigning the oaths to the *prodikasiai*. Before the first *prodikasia* the basileus would probably not know what kind of defence the accused man proposed to make; he would thus not know whether the case ought to be allotted to the Delphinion court (for allotment of a case to that court depended on the nature of the defence, not on the nature of the charge). So the allotment of a case to a particular court is likely to have been made after the holding of the *prodikasiai*, not before. Demosthenes says that the oaths were taken on the Areopagos and at the Palladion for cases tried by those courts (D.23.67, 71); this implies that the oaths were sworn after the cases had been allotted to individual courts. In the speech *On the Chorister* the bystanders at the trial are said to hear the administering of the oaths (Ant.6.14). I conclude that the oaths were sworn at the trial, and probably not also at the *prodikasiai*.

At what stages in the trial did the accuser and the accused swear their oaths? An answer to this question is given in *Lexeis Rhetorikai*, but unfortunately the text is confused or corrupt. In Bekker's edition it runs thus.

> *Lexeis Rhetorikai* in *Lex.Seg.*239.23-30. διωμοσία· ὅρκος ἐστίν, ὃν ὤμνυον οἱ φόνου ἀγῶνα διώκοντες ἢ φεύγοντες. ἀμφότεροι γὰρ ὤμνυον μετὰ τὸ εἰπεῖν τὸν παρόντα λόγον, ἦ μὴν ἀληθῆ κατηγορηκέναι καὶ δικαίως, ὁ δὲ ἦ μὴν ἀληθῆ ἀπολελογῆσθαι καὶ δικαίως. ὤμνυον δὲ καὶ πρὶν εἰπεῖν τὸν αὐτὸν ὅρκον ἀμφότεροι ἐπενεχθείσης ἤδη τῆς ψήφου, εἰ μὴ δικαίως νενικηκέναι, ἐξώλειαν ἑαυτῷ ἐπαρώμενος, εἰ ἐξηπάτησεν.

In the last sentence ' after the vote had already been held ' cannot belong to the same clause as ' before speaking ', and the infinitive νενικηκέναι cannot be the verb of a clause beginning with εἰ. The correct reading here is probably something like that suggested by Mederle 23 note 3 : καὶ ἐπενεχθείσης ἤδη τῆς ψήφου ὁ νικῶν ἦ μὴν δικαίως νενικηκέναι. In the middle sentence ὁ μὲν must be either expressed or understood before the first ἦ μὴν. The passage may then be translated as follows.

' *Diomosia* : this is an oath sworn by those accusing or accused in a case of homicide. Both swore after speaking the present [?] speech, one that his accusation had been true and just, the other that his defence had been true and just. They both swore the same oath before speaking ; and after the vote had already been held the winner swore that he had won the case justly, invoking destruction on himself if he had been guilty of deception.'

The passage thus accords with the other evidence that both the accuser and the accused swore at the beginning of the trial before making their speeches (especially D.23.71 : πρῶτον μὲν διωμοσία, δεύτερον δὲ λόγος), and that the winner swore again after the verdict (Ais.2.87). The remaining puzzle is the swearing after ' the present speech '. The word ' present ' seems to have little point. Mederle, followed by Bonner and Smith ii 171, reads τὸν πρότερον λόγον, ' the first speech ', but I do not know what authority this reading has. There is no other evidence for the swearing of oaths either at the end of the first speech made by each party, or at the end of the final speeches, before the verdict. But the lexicographer seems to distinguish this swearing clearly from the oath of the winner after the verdict, and it is therefore not plausible to dismiss it (as Lipsius 833 note 17 does) as having no other authority than Ais.2.87. The mystery must remain unsolved.

An oath had also to be sworn by witnesses in homicide trials. This is stated by the accused man in the Herodes case, in the passage in which he contrasts what is actually being done in the present case with what ought to be done under the normal procedure for homicide trials.

Ant.5.12. ἀνώμοτοι δὲ οἱ μάρτυρες καταμαρτυροῦσι, δέον αὐτοὺς τὸν αὐτὸν ὅρκον σοὶ διομοσαμένους καὶ ἁπτομένους τῶν σφαγίων καταμαρτυρεῖν ἐμοῦ. 'The witnesses are giving evidence against me unsworn, although they ought to swear the same oath as you and touch the sacrificial victims before giving evidence against me.'

In Isok.18.56 Kallimakhos is said to have committed perjury (ἐπιορκῶν) at the trial of Kratinos; this confirms that at a homicide trial an oath was sworn by a witness for the prosecution. In the speech *Against the Stepmother* there are references to the oath of a witness for the defence.

Ant.1.8. πῶς οὖν εὔορκα ἀντομωμοκὼς ἔσται φάσκων εὖ εἰδέναι; 'If he says he knows well [that his mother did not kill her husband], how will his statement be true to the oath sworn by him against me?'

Ant.1.28. θαυμάζω δὲ ἔγωγε τῆς τόλμης τοῦ ἀδελφοῦ καὶ τῆς διανοίας, τὸ διομόσασθαι ὑπὲρ τῆς μητρὸς εὖ εἰδέναι μὴ πεποιηκέναι ταῦτα. 'I am amazed at my brother's audacity. I do not know what he is thinking of, to take the oath for his mother, that he knows well that she did not do this.'

The swearer here is the son of the accused woman, who is conducting her defence for her (Ant.1.5). But that does not mean that the oath he swears is the oath of the accused, as some have thought (e.g. Maidment 19). Though women did not make speeches in court, they did swear oaths (compare the oath of Plangon in D.39.3-4, 40.10-11). So the accused woman will have sworn her own oath, and the son's oath is that of a supporter or witness. The use of the verb ἀντομνύναι in Ant.1.8 is a little surprising, since this verb is not elsewhere used in connexion with homicide cases. But perhaps (as Mederle 14 suggests) it does not mean that the oath was called *antomosia*, but is merely equivalent to ἀντι-διόμνυσθαι, ' swear the oath against ' ; so there is no need to conclude (as Wijnberg 69 does) that two oaths were sworn, first one called *diomosia* and afterwards another called *antomosia*. The wording in Ant.1.28 shows that swearing the oath and saying that he knew his mother did not commit the homicide were one act, not two ; therefore the future tense in Ant.1.8 shows that the oath (and not merely the statement of knowledge) was still in the future when these words were spoken ; and this proves that witnesses took the oath not at the beginning of the trial but when they gave their evidence.

Thus witnesses in a case of homicide had to swear that the accused committed the homicide, or that he did not commit it. This goes further than the oath demanded of a witness in a modern law-court, to the effect that he will tell the truth as far as he knows it, and of course it goes a very great distance further than no oath at all. Yet in other kinds of trial in Athens, sometimes at least, no oath at all was demanded of witnesses. So the oath demanded in homicide cases indicates exceptional concern that convictions should be based only on true and sincere evidence.

XI

WITNESSES

In trials for offences other than homicide witnesses originally gave their evidence orally, but at some date in the first half of the fourth century (G. M. Calhoun, in *TAPA* l [1919] 190-3, argued for 378/7) a law was made requiring witnesses to give their evidence in writing beforehand, and at the trial merely appear and give assent to it. (The evidence that there was a law is D.45.44; many fourth-century speeches refer to the reading of witnesses' statements.) But at a later date an orator mentions a witness in a case of wounding who gave evidence on the Areopagos orally (D.40.33 : πρὸς τὴν ἐξ ᾿Αρείου πάγου βουλὴν εἶπεν τὴν ἀλήθειαν πᾶσαν). From this it has been argued by Bonner (*CP* vii 450-1) that evidence was always given orally on the Areopagos in cases of homicide too, and also in the other special homicide courts. These are large deductions from the single word εἶπεν in D.40.33. But nothing disproves Bonner's contention, and it may well be right.

A witness in a homicide case could not just state what he knew without giving his support to either side. He had to be either for or against the accused, and he had to take an oath either that the accused committed the homicide or that he did not commit it. (On the oath, see pages 98-100.) But a speaker would not necessarily call any witnesses at all. In the speech *Against the Stepmother* (Ant.1) no witnesses for the prosecution are called, perhaps because the accuser could find no one willing to swear that the accused was guilty (as is suggested by Gernet *Antiphon* 36-7).

It has sometimes been thought that women, children, and slaves were permitted to appear as witnesses in homicide trials, although they were not allowed to do so in other kinds of case. This is a vexed question. Among the more recent discussions of it, or of aspects of it, are those of Bonner in *CP* i and vii, Lipsius 873-4, Bonner and Smith ii 221-9, and Gernet *Droit et société* 151-5. I think that it is insoluble, for lack of evidence. I shall not make a detailed review and criticism of the various attempts of scholars to solve it ; instead I shall review the passages of the Attic orators and of Plato which have been adduced as evidence, and explain why I believe they provide no basis for a solution.

1. Ant.2c.4. οὐκ ὀρθῶς δὲ τὴν τοῦ ἀκολούθου μαρτυρίαν ἄπιστον λέγουσιν εἶναι. οὐ γὰρ ἐπὶ ταῖς τοιαύταις μαρτυρίαις βασανίζονται, ἀλλ᾽ ἐλεύθεροι ἀφίενται. 'They are not right in saying that the slave's evidence is untrustworthy. For evidence of this kind they [i.e. slaves] are not tortured, but are given their freedom.'

What is supposed to have happened in this imaginary case is that the killed man's slave, the only person to see the killer, was himself fatally wounded, but survived just long enough to tell those who found him the name of one of the killers (Ant.2a.9). So μαρτυρία is not used here in its technical sense of testimony given at a trial, and there is no question of a slave's appearance in court. The ' evidence ' is simply an informal statement by the slave of what he saw.

2. Ant.5.36. ἐχρῆν μὲν γὰρ αὐτούς, ὡς ἐγὼ νομίζω, ἐνθάδε παρέχοντας τὸν μηνυτὴν αὐτὸν ἀπελέγχειν ἐμέ, καὶ αὐτῷ τούτῳ χρῆσθαι ἀγωνίσματι, ἐμφανῆ παρέχοντας τὸν ἄνδρα καὶ κελεύοντας βασανίζειν, ἀλλὰ μὴ ἀποκτεῖναι. ' In my opinion they ought to have produced the informer himself in Athens to prove their case against me ; and

this is precisely how they ought to have settled the case, by producing the man in public and challenging me to examine him under torture, not by putting him to death.'

The speaker is defending himself against the charge that he killed Herodes.   But the case is not, legally, a homicide case.   The speaker is being accused as a ' wrongdoer ' (Ant. 5.9 : κακοῦργος ἐνδεδειγμένος), so that the case is being heard not on the Areopagos but by an ordinary heliastic court.   It is true that earlier in the speech (Ant.5.8-16) he has argued that the procedure for homicide cases ought to have been followed in this case.   But since it has not in fact been followed, it is quite natural that now, in a later part of the speech, the method which he suggests for obtaining the slave's evidence is the method used in cases other than those of homicide, and consequently the passage does not prove that the examination of slaves under torture was normal in homicide cases.

  3. Ant.5.48.   καίτοι οὐδὲ οἱ τοὺς δεσπότας ἀποκτεί- ναντες, ἐὰν ἐπ' αὐτοφώρῳ ληφθῶσιν, οὐδ' οὗτοι ἀποθνή- σκουσιν ὑπ' αὐτῶν τῶν προσηκόντων, ἀλλὰ παραδιδόασιν αὐτοὺς τῇ ἀρχῇ κατὰ νόμους ὑμετέρους πατρίους.   εἴπερ γὰρ καὶ μαρτυρεῖν ἔξεστι δούλῳ κατὰ τοῦ [or perhaps we ought to read κατά του] ἐλευθέρου τὸν φόνον, καὶ τῷ δε- σπότῃ, ἂν δοκῇ, ἐπεξελθεῖν ὑπὲρ τοῦ δούλου, καὶ ἡ ψῆφος ἴσον δύναται τῷ δοῦλον ἀποκτείναντι καὶ τῷ ἐλεύθερον, εἰκός τοι καὶ ψῆφον γενέσθαι περὶ αὐτοῦ ἦν, καὶ μὴ ἄκριτον ἀποθανεῖν αὐτὸν ὑφ' ὑμῶν.   ' Yet not even those who kill their own masters, and are caught in the act, are put to death by the relatives themselves, but they hand them over to the arkhon in accordance with the traditional laws of Athens.   And if it is permissible both to give evidence for a slave against a free man of his being killed, and for his master, if he thinks fit, to initiate a prosecution on

H

behalf of the slave, and the vote has power equally over one who kills a slave and one who kills a free man, surely it was reasonable that a vote should be held also about him, and not that he should be put to death by you without trial.'

The speaker is still discussing the slave who has been summarily executed by his opponents, and he argues that even a slave should not be put to death without trial. As evidence for his argument he quotes the rule : μαρτυρεῖν ἔξεστι δούλῳ κατὰ τοῦ ἐλευθέρου τὸν φόνον. Most scholars take δούλῳ with ἔξεστι and make the sentence mean ' it is permissible for a slave to give evidence against a free man about a killing '. This translation is wrong, for two reasons. First, it ignores the article τὸν. Secondly (and far more important), it does not suit the context. The speaker is talking about the killing of a slave ; he is saying that killing a slave is an offence for which a free man may be tried. Talk about evidence given by a slave would be quite irrelevant. It is necessary to take δούλῳ as the indirect object of μαρτυρεῖν, in the sense ' in support of a slave ', ' in vengeance for a slave ', and to take τὸν as ' his ' (the slave's). (This grammatical construction with μαρτυρεῖν is perfectly normal. A witness who gives evidence against a killer may be regarded as giving evidence in support of the killed man, just as the prosecutor is acting in support of the killed man ; compare ὑπὲρ τοῦ δούλου later in this same sentence. With μαρτυρεῖν the dative is regular for the person in whose support evidence is given, e.g. D.33.37 : μαρτυρήσει τις αὐτῷ κατ' ἐμοῦ, ' someone will give evidence in favour of him and against me '.) When a slave is killed, his master may prosecute the killer, and others may give evidence against the killer. So this passage does not show that a slave could appear in court as a witness.

4. Ant.6.19. . . . τὰ πραχθέντα φανερῶς ἅπαντα πραχ-
θῆναι καὶ ἐναντίον μαρτύρων πολλῶν, καὶ ἀνδρῶν καὶ παί-
δων, καὶ ἐλευθέρων καὶ δούλων, . . . '. . . that all that
was done was done openly and in the presence of many
witnesses, men and boys, free persons and slaves, . . .'

Ant.6.22. . . . ἃ μέντοι αἰτιῷτο καὶ διαβάλλοι, ῥᾳδίως
ἐξελεγχθήσοιτο ψευδόμενος· εἶεν γὰρ οἱ συνειδότες πολλοί,
καὶ ἐλεύθεροι καὶ δοῦλοι, καὶ νεώτεροι καὶ πρεσβύτεροι,
. . . '. . . but that his accusations and slanders would
easily be proved to be lies ; for there were many who
knew what happened, free persons and slaves, young and
old, . . .'

The word μάρτυς, like the English ' witness', can be used
in two different ways. It may mean a person who sees
something happen. Or it may mean a person who appears
in court to give evidence about something. Often of course
the two senses overlap, because the same person sees an
event and afterwards gives evidence about it in court. But
often they are quite distinct. When Plato makes Sokrates
say that Agathon's wisdom was recently seen in the theatre
by more than thirty thousand witnesses (Pl.*Smp*.175e : ἐν
μάρτυσι τῶν Ἑλλήνων πλέον ἢ τρισμυρίοις), he does not mean
that all those people gave, or might give, evidence in a law-
court, and his statement proves nothing about the legal
status of various individual members of the audience ; he
simply means that thirty thousand people saw the play.
Similarly here, the khoregos means that many people saw
Diodotos take the drink which poisoned him. These passages do not refer to a trial, and do not prove that boys and
slaves could give evidence in court.

Ant.1.30 (quoted on page 1), where slaves are called
μάρτυρας, is to be explained in the same way.

5. In Lysias 1 Euphiletos claims that he killed Eratos-

thenes lawfully, because he caught him in adultery with his wife. He says that on the night in question his slave-girl warned him that Eratosthenes was with his wife, and admitted him to the room in which they were (Lys.1.23-4). If his story is true, who could better confirm it than the wife and the slave ? Or if it is false, who could better refute it ? Yet the speech contains no statement that either of them was called as a witness ; and so, it has been suggested, this proves that women and slaves could not appear as witnesses.

It proves nothing of the kind. In the first place, the fact that the speech, as we have it, contains no statement that the wife and the slave were called as witnesses does not in itself prove that they were not called. Some witnesses of the killing were called at the end of section 29 ; the speech gives no indication who these witnesses were, and they may possibly have included the wife or the slave or both. In the second place, if it is true that neither the wife nor the slave was called, perhaps that is because neither Euphiletos nor his accusers wished to call them. Euphiletos may have feared that his wife and slave might try to deny that his wife had committed adultery even though she actually had. His accusers may have feared that his wife and slave might be afraid to contradict Euphiletos even though he was really guilty. So the speech does not show that women and slaves could never appear as witnesses.

6. In D.47.69-70 (quoted on page 13) the exegetai give advice to the trierarkhos. In the first part of their advice they say : ' Since you were not present yourself, but only your wife and children, and there are no others to act as witnesses for you, . . .'. This does not make clear either that the wife and children could act as witnesses or that they could not. A few lines later the exegetai mention the possibility that the trierarkhos and his wife and children might

take an oath at the Palladion. It is not quite clear whether the wife and children would appear and swear in person ; a little later the trierarkhos says ψεύσασθαι δὲ πρὸς ὑμᾶς καὶ διομόσασθαι αὐτὸς καὶ τὸν υἱὸν καὶ τὴν γυναῖκα οὐκ ἂν ἐτόλμησα, which appears to mean ' I should not have dared to lie to you and take the oath for myself, my son, and my wife ', and this may perhaps imply that the oath would have been taken only by the trierarkhos on behalf of his family, and not by the wife and children separately. (It is only fair to point out, however, that Dareste and Bonner interpret this sentence differently : ' . . . cause my son and my wife to swear . . .'. See CP i 128 note 3.) But in any case the question here is one of prosecution, not of evidence : was the family to prosecute the killers of the old nurse ? It was normal for a prosecution for homicide to be brought by a family (cf. pages 16-18), and for a number of members of the family to swear the oath for the prosecution, while the accused alone swore the oath for the defence (e.g. Ant.6.16 : διωμόσαντο δὲ οὗτοι μὲν ἀποκτεῖναί με Διόδοτον . . . , ἐγὼ δὲ μὴ ἀποκτεῖναι). So the trierarkhos's wife and children might have taken the oath simply because they were associated with the prosecution, and the passage proves nothing about whether women and children could appear as witnesses.

7. D.59.9. παρασκευασάμενος ἀνθρώπους δούλους καὶ κατασκευάσας ὡς Κυρηναῖοι εἴησαν, προεῖπεν αὐτῷ ἐπὶ Παλλαδίῳ φόνου. 'Procuring some slaves and making out that they were Kyreneans, he [Stephanos] made proclamation to him [Apollodoros] for homicide at the Palladion.'

The false witnesses were really slaves, but were alleged to be Kyreneans. It has been argued (by Bonner and Smith ii 228-9) that this proves that slaves could not appear as witnesses. But it would be equally good, or equally absurd, to say that it proves that no one but Kyreneans could appear as a witness. Why was a Kyrenean disguise chosen ? We do not know, because we have not enough information about the circumstances of the case. But presumably there was some reason; and, for all we know, the thing that mattered to Stephanos may have been that the witnesses should appear to be Kyreneans, not that they should not appear to be slaves. So this passage provides no ground for the view that slaves could never appear as witnesses.

8. Pl.*Laws* 937a-b. γυναικὶ δ' ἐξέστω ἐλευθέρᾳ μαρτυρεῖν καὶ συνηγορεῖν, ἐὰν ὑπὲρ τετταράκοντα ἔτη ᾖ γε-
γονυῖα, καὶ δίκην λαγχάνειν, ἐὰν ἄνανδρος ᾖ· ζῶντος δὲ
ἀνδρὸς ἐξέστω μαρτυρῆσαι μόνον. δούλῃ δὲ καὶ δούλῳ καὶ
παιδὶ φόνου μόνον ἐξέστω μαρτυρεῖν καὶ συνηγορεῖν. ' A
free woman shall be permitted to be a witness and a supporter in court, if she is over forty years of age, and to
bring a case, if she has no husband ; but if she has a husband living, she shall be permitted to be a witness only.
An enslaved woman and an enslaved man and a child shall
be permitted to be a witness and a supporter in court for
homicide only.'

Bonner has argued (*CP* i 130-1 ; cf. Bonner and Smith ii 222) that this provision of Plato's affords ' a striking confirmation of the view that women were competent witnesses in homicide cases ' in Athenian law. He maintains that Plato's rules imply that all free women could be witnesses in homicide cases, since otherwise an adult free woman under forty would lack a privilege allowed to slave-women and girls, and that Plato could not have allowed this implication to remain unexpressed unless it was part of the existing practice of Athenian law. Two objections may be made. First, it is likely that Plato regarded a woman under forty as a minor (παῖς), so that for him the category of ' adult women under forty ' did not exist (cf. *Laws* 785b, 932c).   Secondly, it is not clear that Plato's legal system is intended to be perfectly complete and without loopholes, so that any argument from his silence is precarious.

Scholars often dislike to confess ignorance.   But to the question ' Were women, children, and slaves allowed to appear in court to give evidence in homicide cases ? ' the only proper answer, unless further information is discovered, is that we do not know.

XII

PENALTIES AND PARDON

WHEN the oaths and speeches were finished, there was no summing-up or advice to the jury by the basileus or any other impartial person, nor did the jury have any time for deliberation ; they voted immediately. There is no information about the voting procedure in homicide trials, but the principle that a tie in the voting meant acquittal seems to have applied in homicide courts as in others (A.*Eu*.741, 752-3). If the accused was acquitted, it was customary for him to make a sacrifice to the August goddesses (Σεμναί) at their sanctuary near the Areopagos (Paus.1.28.6). If he was convicted, he could not appeal (Ant.6.3 : ἔστι μὲν γὰρ περὶ τοῦ τοιούτου μία δίκη, ' for this kind of case there is only one trial ' ; cf. 6.6) ; he at once became subject to the penalty fixed by law.

Demosthenes lists in his speech *Against Meidias* the various kinds of penalty imposed for intentional homicide, and tries to draw a sharp distinction between them and the treatment of unintentional homicide.

> D.21.43. οἱ φονικοὶ [sc. νόμοι] τοὺς μὲν ἐκ προνοίας ἀποκτιννύντας θανάτῳ καὶ ἀειφυγίᾳ καὶ δημεύσει τῶν ὑπαρχόντων ζημιοῦσι, τοὺς δ' ἀκουσίως αἰδέσεως καὶ φιλανθρωπίας πολλῆς ἠξίωσαν. ' The homicide laws punish deliberate killers with death, perpetual exile, and confiscation of property, but for unintentional killers they allow pardon and very sympathetic treatment.'

When a killer was condemned to death, his accuser was

permitted to watch the execution, but not to carry it out himself. This is stated by Demosthenes in his speech *Against Aristokrates*.

D.23.69. ἂν δὲ δόξῃ τὰ δίκαι' ἐγκαλεῖν καὶ ἕλῃ τὸν δεδρακότα τοῦ φόνου, οὐδ' οὕτω κύριος γίγνεται τοῦ ἁλόντος, ἀλλ' ἐκείνου μὲν οἱ νόμοι κύριοι κολάσαι καὶ οἷς προστέτακται, τῷ δ' ἐπιδεῖν διδόντα δίκην ἔξεστιν, ἣν ἔταξ' ὁ νόμος, τὸν ἁλόντα, πέρα δ' οὐδὲν τούτου. 'If it is decided that his accusation is just and he gains a conviction of the killer, even so he has no power over the convicted man. The laws, and those whose office it is, have power to punish the convicted man; the accuser is permitted to watch him paying the penalty fixed by law, but not to do any more than this.'

The phrase 'the penalty fixed by law' is not explicit; but it can hardly refer to exile (how would the accuser watch the condemned man paying the penalty of exile?), and it may be assumed to be a euphemistic expression for execution. The method of execution used for homicide seems to have been ἀποτυμπανίζειν, killing by means of a *tympanon*. Two problems arise in connexion with it: how exactly did the method work? and was this the method used for persons condemned for homicide? The first of these is not really a legal problem, and in any case is probably insoluble on the evidence at present available; I shall therefore not attempt to discuss it in detail, but shall merely indicate what are the principal accounts that have been given. The only ancient author who makes a serious attempt to explain the method is a late lexicographer.

Synagoge Lexeon Khresimon in *Lex.Seg.*438.12-15. ἀποτυμπανίσαι· οὐχ ἁπλῶς τὸ ἀποκτεῖναι, ἀλλὰ τυμπάνοις ἀποκτεῖναι. τύμπανον δέ ἐστι ξύλον ὥσπερ σκύταλον. τὸ γὰρ παλαιὸν ξύλοις ἀνῄρουν τοὺς κατακρίτους, ὕστερον δ' ἔδοξε τῷ ξίφει. '*Apotympanisai* : not just "kill", but "kill with *tympana* ". A *tympanon* is a piece of wood, like a club. In ancient times they used to execute the condemned with pieces of wood, but later they decided to do it with the sword.'

On the basis of this account some have thought (e.g. Lipsius 77 note 101) that the *tympanon* was a club with which the condemned man was beaten to death. But Keramopoullos (in his book entitled Ὁ ἀποτυμπανισμός) argues on the basis of archaeological discoveries at Phaleron that the *tympanon* was a piece of wood fixed in an upright position, and that the condemned man was fastened to it by five iron bands around his neck, wrists, and ankles, and left to die of exposure and starvation. Bonner and Smith (ii 279-82) modify the view of Keramopoullos by supposing that the iron collar was tightened, by means of nails, so as to cause death by strangulation. It may be unwise to ignore completely the account given in the *Synagoge Lexeon Khresimon*, as they do; but it is perhaps possible to reconcile their explanation with the lexicographer's, if we assume that ' like a club ' means only that the *tympanon* was wooden, not that it was shaped or used like a club. Bonner and Smith's account may then be tentatively accepted as a plausible suggestion.

Gernet (*REG* xxxvii 265 note 3) has expressed doubt whether the *tympanon* was the normal method of execution for homicide, but ' nous restons dans une ignorance totale ' is an unnecessarily pessimistic statement of the position. When Menestratos was condemned to death and executed by means of the *tympanon* (Lys.13.56), he had probably not been condemned at one of the special homicide courts, but had been prosecuted by *apagoge* (see chapter XIII). But the speaker explicitly says that he was condemned as a killer (ὡς ἀνδροφόνον ὄντα) ; and there is no need to doubt that this was the normal method of executing killers, since Demosthenes, speaking of the attacks made on him by Meidias, says that Meidias thought it right that he should ' be exiled for bloodshed, and very nearly be nailed up ' (D.21.105 : προσηλῶσθαι). Not an easy death, as he remarks elsewhere through the mouth of Diodoros (D.24.7).

When exile was the penalty for intentional homicide, it lasted for life. This is shown by the word ἀειφυγίᾳ in D.21.43 (quoted on page 110) ; and the accused man in the *First Tetralogy* seems to expect that if he is exiled he will remain in exile in his old age.

Ant.2b.9. ἐὰν δὲ νῦν καταληφθεὶς ἀποθάνω, ἀνόσια ὀνείδη τοῖς παισὶν ὑπολείψω, ἢ φυγὼν γέρων καὶ ἄπολις ὢν ἐπὶ ξενίας πτωχεύσω. ' If I am now convicted and put to death, I shall leave behind for my children the disgrace of an unholy deed ; or if I go into exile, I shall be an old man without a city, a beggar in a foreign land.'

But this passage, like D.21.43, raises the question : if death and exile were alternative penalties for intentional homicide, how was it decided which of the two was to be imposed in any individual case ? Modern notions of capital and non-capital murder may suggest the idea that death was imposed for the most serious type of intentional homicide and perpetual exile for a less serious type, and that the Areopagos (or the court at the Delphinion or the court in Phreatto) would decide which penalty was appropriate in each individual case. But in fact there is no indication in the ancient authorities that these courts ever made this kind of distinction.

So it is better to seek an explanation in the rule that an accused man might, if he wished, go into exile after making the first of the two speeches in his defence. It was the normal practice at a homicide trial for each party to make two speeches, in the order : accuser, accused, accuser, accused. This arrangement is exemplified in the three *Tetralogies* attributed to Antiphon. Each *Tetralogy* consists of four model speeches written for an imaginary case to illustrate methods of stating arguments and rebutting them. There is no instance of a real homicide case from which more than a single speech is extant ; but that does not mean that the *Tetralogies* do not reflect real practice accurately. In the speech *On the Chorister*, for example, the accused man refers to the second speech of the accuser, which has not yet been made (Ant.6.14). The survival of only single speeches from real cases is not necessarily just accidental. It may be because a speaker would generally prepare his first speech in writing before the trial, but would often extemporize his second speech in answer to the arguments produced by his opponent, so that when the trial was over only the first speech was available in writing for publication.

In Ant.5.13 and D.23.69 it is stated that anyone accused of homicide was permitted to go into exile, if he wished, after making the first of his two speeches, and neither the accuser nor anyone else might prevent him from doing so. (Polyd. 8.117 adds that this course was not open to a person who had killed his parents. There is no other evidence to confirm or refute this exception.) The rule is illustrated in the *Third Tetralogy*. There the fourth speech is supposed to be delivered by a relative of the accused, and he begins by saying that the accused himself has withdrawn, ' not declaring himself guilty, but fearing the zeal of the accusers ' (Ant.4d.1). This shows how to interpret the sentence just quoted from Ant.2b.9. The alternatives which the speaker contemplates are these : either he may stay in court and risk being condemned to death, or he may leave Athens at the end of his present speech (which is the first of his two speeches) and thus condemn himself to banishment for the rest of his life.

To leave to the accused man the choice between death and exile may appear a humane custom, especially to modern opponents of capital punishment. But in practice the choice must often have been fiendishly hard, because it had to be made before the court gave its verdict. To be sure of avoiding death, a man had to go into exile without waiting to see whether the jury would acquit him. If he waited for the verdict at the end of the trial and then was found guilty, it was too late to go into exile. But if he went into exile before the end of the trial, the jurors would probably take his flight as a sign that he had a guilty conscience and expected to be condemned, and so they would be more inclined to condemn him than if he had stayed in Athens. (Compare And.1.3 : ' When men declare themselves guilty by refusing to stay to face trial, you very naturally make the same decision about them as they have made about themselves'.) The system contained a large element of gambling. This is enough to show that its origin lay not in a humane belief that a guilty man should be allowed to choose exile in place of death, but in the fact that it was not practicable in early times for the law to pursue a man beyond the boundaries of the state, or else possibly in the belief that the state was not polluted by a man who had left it. In other words, the Athenians' reaction (originally at least) when a killer went into exile was not ' He does not deserve any severer penalty ', but ' It is hopeless to try to catch him now ' or ' We are rid of him ; so why should we care ? '

Another penalty inflicted for intentional homicide was confiscation of property. This is included in the list in

D.21.43 (quoted on page 110), and it is also mentioned by Euphiletos, the killer of Eratosthenes, in his peroration.

Lys.1.50. ἐγὼ γὰρ νῦν καὶ περὶ τοῦ σώματος καὶ περὶ τῶν χρημάτων καὶ περὶ τῶν ἄλλων ἁπάντων κινδυνεύω. 'I now have at stake myself and my property and everything else.'

In the *Ath.Pol.* it is stated that the sellers of state property (πωληταί) sold 'the properties of those who are in exile from the Areopagos'.

*Ath.Pol.*47.2. καὶ τὰς οὐσίας τῶν ἐξ Ἀρείου πάγου φευγόντων καὶ τῶν ἄλλων ἐναντίον τῆς βουλῆς πωλοῦσιν, κατακυροῦσι δ' οἱ θ' ἄρχοντες. 'They sell the properties of those who are in exile from the Areopagos and the rest in the presence of the council; the nine arkhons ratify the sales.'

Polydeukes too says (8.99) that they sold 'the properties of those who have gone into exile from the Areopagos after the first speech'; and Demosthenes more briefly says that the possessions of deliberate killers in exile were confiscated (D.23.45 : τῶν γὰρ ἐκ προνοίας [sc. ἀνδροφόνων τῶν ἐξεληλυθότων] δεδήμευται τὰ ὄντα). These three passages show that confiscation was imposed in addition to exile, not as an alternative.

When a killer was executed, was his property confiscated as well? Glotz *La solidarité* 515-20 and Treston 220-1 maintain that it was not. (Treston makes an exception of cases of parricide; but the anecdote related by Cicero *Pro Roscio Amerino* 70 and Diogenes Laertios 1.59, that Solon fixed no penalty for parricide because he thought no one would commit it, indicates that in Athens parricide had no different penalty from other kinds of homicide.) In D.24.7 Diodoros says that if he had been found guilty of killing his father 'not only should I have been deprived of my possessions, but I should not even have remained alive '. In the sentence just quoted from Lys.1.50 Euphiletos says that he has at stake himself and his property. The word σῶμα, which I have translated ' myself ', can refer either to a person's life (e.g. And.1.4-5, 105, Lys.5.1) or to his rights as a citizen (e.g. And.1.74, 123, D.51.12). Euphiletos would lose his rights as a citizen if he went into exile. But, the charge against him being one of intentional homicide, he would go into exile only if he went voluntarily after his first speech. His speech as we have it contains no other hint that he contemplates doing this, and so it is more likely that σῶμα here means ' life '. And if he was staying in court after his first speech, so that the penalty if he was convicted would be death, and yet still had his property at stake, it follows that confiscation of property was imposed on intentional killers who were executed as well as on those who went into exile. (Glotz bases his argument on Ant.2b.9 and *Ath.Pol.*47.2, in which he thinks that the fact that confiscation accompanied death, if true, should have been made clear. But the silence of these two passages, or rather the vagueness of ἀνόσια ὀνείδη in the first and of τῶν ἄλλων in the second, is insufficient to counter the evidence of Lys.1.50 and D.24.7.)

The penalty for unintentional homicide was less severe, though the words used in D.21.43, ' pardon and very sympathetic treatment ', are an over-lenient account of it. A large part of the principal law about unintentional homicide is preserved on a stone on which it was reinscribed in 409/8. (I am not here concerned with the difficult questions why it was reinscribed, and why the law about intentional homicide does not appear on the same stone. The most recent discussion of these problems is that of Harrison in *CQ* xi [1961] 3-5.) It may safely be assumed that the law in this inscription remained valid throughout the age of the orators, because in the introductory lines of the inscription it is called ' the law of Drakon about homicide ' (*IG* i² 115.4-5), and there is adequate evidence that after 408 the Athenians continued to use what they thought (correctly or not) were the laws of Drakon about homicide (And.1.83, D.20.158, 23.51, 47.71). The inscription is badly mutilated, and many lines of it are entirely or largely illegible. Some clauses of the law are quoted in D.23.28, 23.37, 43.57 ; these passages are further evidence that the law remained in force in the fourth century, and they also enable many missing parts of the inscription to be restored. With supplements, the main part of it runs thus.

> *IG* i² 115.11-32.
>
> καὶ ἐὰμ [μ]ὲ 'κ [π]ρονο[ία]ς [κ]τ[ένει τίς τινα, φεύγεν, δ]ι-
> κάζεν δὲ τὸς βασιλέας αἰτ[ι]ô[ν] φό[νο] ἒ [ἐάν τις αἰτιᾶται hος
>   βου]λ-
> εύσαντα· τὸς [δ]ὲ ἐφέτας διαγν[ôναι. αἰδέσασθαι δ' ἐὰμ μὲν
>   πατὲρ] ἒ-
> ι ἒ ἀδελφὸ[ς] ἒ hυês, hάπα[ντας], ἒ τὸ[ν κ]ο[λύοντα κρατên·
>   ἐὰν δὲ μὲ ho]ῦ-
> 15 τοι ὂσ[ι, μ]έ[χ]ρ' ἀ[ν]εφ[σι]ότ[ε]τος κ[αὶ ἀνεφσιô, ἐὰν hά-
>   παντες αἰδέσα]σ-
> θαι ἐθέλοσ[ι], τὸν hό[ρκ]ον [ὀμόσαντας· ἐὰν δὲ τούτον μεδ'
>   hês êι, κτέ]-
> νει δὲ ἄκο[ν], γ[ν]ôσ[ι δ]ὲ h[οι πεν]τ[έκοντα καὶ hês hοι ἐφέται
>   ἄκοντα]
> κτêναι, ἐσέσθ[ο]ν δέκ[α hοι φράτερες ἐὰν ἐθέλοσιν· τούτος δ]ὲ
>   [ho]-
> ι πεντέκο[ν]τ[α καὶ] hês ἀρ[ι]σ[τίνδεν hαιρέσθον. υυ καὶ hοι
>   πρό]τε[ρ]-
> 20 ον κτέ[ν]α[ντες ἐν τ]ô[ιδε τôι θεσμôι ἐνεχέσθον. προειπên δὲ
>   τôι] ϙ-

τέ[ναντι ἐν ἀ]γορ[ᾶι ἐντ]ὸ[ς ἀνεφσιότετος καὶ ἀνεφσιô· συν-
διόκε]ν
δὲ [καὶ ἀνε]φσ[ιὸς καὶ ἀνεφσιôν παῖδας καὶ γαμβρὸς καὶ πεν-
θερὸ]ς [κ]-
αὶ φ[ρά]τ[ε]ρ[ας ....³⁹...............]ι-
ος ..φο...⁶...φ[...........²¹........... τὸς πεντέκοντα κα]ὶ
25 ἕνα [...............⁴²............... φ]όνο
ἑ[λ]οσ[ι ....³⁵............... ἐὰν δέ τις] τ-
ὸ[ν ἀνδροφόνον κτένει ἒ αἴτιος ἒι φόνο, ἀπεχόμενον ἀγορᾶ]ς
[ἐφ]ο-
ρί[α]ς [καὶ ἄθλον καὶ ἱερὸν Ἀμφικτυονικôν, ὅσπερ τὸν Ἀθε-
ναῖ]ον [κ]-
[τέναντα, ἐν τοῖς αὐτοῖς ἐνέχεσθαι· διαγιγνόσκεν δὲ τὸς ἐφ]έ-
τα[ς].
30 [τὸς δὲ ἀνδροφόνος ἐχσεῖναι ἀποκτένεν καὶ ἀπάγεν ἐν] τê[ι]
ἐμε[δ]-
[απêι, λυμαίνεσθαι δὲ μέ, μεδὲ ἀποινᾶν, ἒ διπλôν ὀφέλεν ὅσ]ον
[ἂν κ]-
[αταβλάφσει — —

'And anyone who kills not deliberately is to go into
exile ; the basileis are to hold trials for accusations of
homicide, or if anyone accuses anyone of *bouleusis*, and
the ephetai are to decide. Pardon is to be granted, if there
is a father or brother or sons, by all, or whoever opposes
15 is to prevail; and if these do not exist, by relatives as far
as the degree of cousin's son and cousin, if all are willing
to grant pardon, after swearing the oath ; and if there is
none of these, and the killing is unintentional, and the
fifty-one, the ephetai, decide that the killing was unintentional, ten members of the phratry shall admit if they are
willing ; these the fifty-one shall select according to rank.
20 Those who killed previously shall be bound by this enact-
ment. Relatives within the degree of cousin's son and
cousin are to make proclamation to the killer in the agora ;

I

the prosecution is to be shared by cousins, sons of cousins,
sons-in-law, fathers-in-law, and members of the phratry
25 . . . the fifty-one . . . convict of homicide . . . anyone who kills the slayer or is responsible for his being
killed, as long as he keeps away from the frontier and
games and Amphiktyonic rites, is to be liable to the same
treatment as one who kills an Athenian, and the ephetai
30 are to decide. It is to be lawful to kill and to arrest slayers
within the country, but not to maltreat them, nor to demand compensation, or the offender must pay double
the amount of his offence . . .'

Some other details emerge from the passage in which
Demosthenes argues that the decree of Aristokrates contravenes existing laws about the court at the Palladion.

D.23.72   τί οὖν ὁ νόμος κελεύει; τὸν ἁλόντ' ἐπ' ἀκου-
σίῳ φόνῳ ἔν τισιν εἰρημένοις χρόνοις ἀπελθεῖν τακτὴν ὁδόν,
καὶ φεύγειν ἕως ἂν αἰδέσηταί τις [App. Francfurtana : τινα
codd.] τῶν ἐν γένει τοῦ πεπονθότος. τηνικαῦτα δ' ἥκειν
δέδωκεν ἔστιν ὃν τρόπον, οὐχ ὃν ἂν τύχῃ, ἀλλὰ καὶ θῦσαι
καὶ καθαρθῆναι καὶ ἄλλ' ἄττα διείρηκεν ἃ χρὴ ποιῆσαι. ' And
what does the law ordain ? That the man convicted for
unintentional homicide shall depart within a certain specified period by a fixed route, and shall remain in exile until
one of the relatives of the dead man pardons him' [the
precise text of this phrase is uncertain, but the general
sense is not in doubt]. ' Then it allows him to return in a
particular manner, not just at random ; it specifies sacrifice, cleansing, and certain other actions which he must
perform.'

These passages, eked out by a few references elsewhere,
provide a coherent account of what happened to a man
found guilty of unintentional homicide. He had to go into
exile; no alternative kind of penalty was permitted. He had

to depart within a specified period and by a specified route, but we have no evidence to show what the period and the route were, nor even whether they were the same in every instance. He had to remain outside the territory of Attica, and he had also to avoid ' games and Amphiktyonic rites '. (Or possibly ' Amphiktyonic games and rites '. Latte maintains, in *RE* xvi 286-7, that the adjective qualifies both nouns, on the grounds that it would have been impossible to exclude a killer from all games in Greece, and that ἀγῶνες unqualified cannot mean only the great national games.) Demosthenes argues (23.40), no doubt rightly, that the aim of this rule was to exclude the killer from ' all things in which his victim shared while he was alive', namely his own country and those festivals and ceremonies which were open to all Greeks.

Provided that he avoided these places, he suffered no other penalty, but was permitted to retain his property and live a free life abroad. We are told that Theophrastos, in Book 13 of his *Laws*, explained that persons convicted of unintentional homicide kept control of their property (Harp. ὅτι οἱ ἁλόντες) ; and Demosthenes quotes a relevant law.

D.23.44. ἐάν τίς τινα τῶν ἀνδροφόνων τῶν ἐξεληλυθό-των, ὧν τὰ χρήματα ἐπίτιμα, πέρα ὅρου ἐλαύνῃ ἢ φέρῃ ἢ ἄγῃ, τὰ ἴσα ὀφείλειν ὅσα περ ἂν ἐν τῇ ἡμεδαπῇ δράσῃ. ' Anyone who beyond the frontier drives or carries or leads an exiled slayer, whose property is not confiscated, is to be liable to the same penalties as if he did so within the country.'

But if he did return to Attica it was lawful for anyone to kill him out of hand. Alternatively he might be proceeded against by *apagoge* or *endeixis*, which were the two normal methods of bringing to justice a person caught exercising a right to which he was not entitled, and if he was found guilty the penalty he could expect was death. This is shown by the word ἀπάγεν in *IG* i² 115.30 (cf. D.23.28), and by a law, quoted by Demosthenes, which exempts persons bringing this kind of prosecution from any possible charge of homicide, on the ground of causing the death of the returned killer by bringing him to justice.

D.23.51.   φόνου δὲ δίκας μὴ εἶναι μηδαμοῦ κατὰ τῶν τοὺς φεύγοντας ἐνδεικνύντων, ἐάν τις κατίῃ ὅποι μὴ ἔξεστιν. ' Trials for homicide are not to be held anywhere of those who prosecute exiles, if anyone returns where it is not lawful for him to return.'

And earlier in the same speech Demosthenes remarks : ' the thesmothetai have authority to punish with death persons exiled for homicide, and you all saw the man arrested by them in the assembly last year ' (D.23.31). But no other way of dealing with an unlawfully returned exile was permitted. Though he might be killed, he might not be maltreated ; and it was specifically forbidden to demand financial compensation from him (*IG* i² 115.31 ; cf. D.23.28).

There is no adequate evidence that any time-limit was normally attached to exile for unintentional homicide. Treston 211-13 takes the view that the normal period of exile was one year. But his only reasons seem to be that Plato specifies one year's exile for unintentional homicide (*Laws* 869e), and that the term ἀπενιαυτεῖν, sometimes used in connexion with unintentional homicide, implies only a single year's exile. (Here Treston might have quoted, though he does not, *Synagoge Lexeon Khresimon* in *Lex.Seg.* 421.20-1 : ἀπενιαυτισμός· φυγὴ ἐπὶ ἐνιαυτὸν διὰ φόνου ἀκούσιον.) But Plato's law is not in itself evidence for Athenian law ; and Plato's own phrase ἐνιαυτοὺς τρεῖς ἀπενιαυτεῖν (*Laws*

868c) proves that ἀπενιαυτεῖν is not necessarily restricted to one year. However, it was possible for the family of the killed man to extend pardon (αἴδεσις) to the killer, and perhaps in some cases the family may have stated in advance how many years must elapse before pardon would be granted.

The family had the right to grant pardon, but was not obliged to do so ; this is shown by the expressions ' if they are willing ' and ' whoever opposes is to prevail ' in the law (*IG* i² 115.14-18). The law specifies which relatives might grant pardon. If the dead man's father survived, or if he left any brothers or sons, they might extend pardon to the killer, but only if they agreed unanimously to do so. One would think that this might make it easier to obtain pardon for killing a man who left, say, no father or brother and only one son than for killing a man who left a father and a large number of brothers and sons. But there is an important difference between the Athenian and the modern attitude to such a difficulty. Whereas in the twentieth century we tend to consider primarily the effect of a penalty on the person on whom it is imposed, the Athenians considered the persons against whom the offence had been committed. A man who killed another offended against all the members of his victim's family ; the larger the family, the greater the number of persons against whom he offended. It is possible that even a brother or son who was a minor was held to be included in the list of relatives who granted pardon, because he had suffered by the killing of his brother or father. However, the law as we have it says nothing about minors explicitly, and it may be that the nearest male relative of a minor acted on the minor's behalf in this as in other matters.

If no father, brother, or son of the killed man survived, pardon might be granted by more distant relatives, as far as the degree of first cousin once removed. (For the degree of relationship, cf. page 18.) Thus if a father, brother, or son had been unyielding, a killer presumably might still hope for pardon when the obstinate relative died. This clause concludes with the phrase ' after swearing the oath '. There is no other evidence to show what this oath was or why it is not mentioned in the clause enabling closer relatives to grant pardon. Possibly the cousins had to swear an oath that no closer relative of the killed man survived; but that is merely a guess.

If no relatives survived even within the degree of first cousin once removed, pardon might be granted by members of the killed man's phratry. Since the phratry was a kind of clan based on family relationship, members of the killed man's phratry would, at least in theory, be distant relatives of his. (But not necessarily in practice. When a non-citizen was granted Athenian citizenship, he was often allowed to choose his own phratry; e.g. *IG* i² 110.15-17. Such a man would as a rule be quite unrelated to the other members of the phratry which he chose.) The procedure was that the fifty-one ephetai selected ten members of the phratry ' according to rank ' (ἀριστίνδην). It is not known what rules were followed for establishing a man's rank within his phratry; it may well be that there were no rules, and that the ephetai had virtually a free choice. The ten members of the phratry selected in this way then decided whether to grant pardon to the killer or not. Stress is laid in this part of the law on the requirement that, for the members of the phratry to be able to grant pardon, the killing must have been unintentional, and a verdict to this effect have been given by the ephetai at the trial. This may possibly imply that relatives within the degrees specified in earlier clauses of the law might grant pardon even in cases in which the killing had not been unintentional. But there is no other evidence to support this inference, and D.21.43 (quoted on page 110) seems to be against it.

When he received pardon, the killer might return to Athens, but he had to follow a special procedure. Demosthenes tells us that it included ' sacrifice, cleansing, and certain other actions ' (D.23.72 : θῦσαι καὶ καθαρθῆναι καὶ ἄλλ' ἄττα), but gives no further details. Other evidence (discussed in detail by Moulinier 87-91) does not tell us any more. In Aiskhylos, Orestes is cleansed at Delphoi by the sacrifice of a pig (A.Eu.283 : καθαρμοῖς χοιροκτόνοις). In Euripides, new-born lambs are brought that Iphigeneia may ' by killing wash out the pollution of killing ' (E.IT1223-4 : νεογνούς τ' ἄρνας, ὡς φόνῳ φόνον μυσαρὸν ἐκνίψω). These two passages show that a sacrifice was regarded by the Athenians as a proper act for the purpose of cleansing a killer from pollution. But poets are not necessarily faithful to precise legal details, and thus it cannot be said that we learn any more about the legal requirements from Aiskhylos and Euripides than from Demosthenes.

Pardon, once granted, could not be revoked.

D.37.59. ἐὰν ἑλών τις ἀκουσίου φόνου καὶ σαφῶς ἐπιδείξας μὴ καθαρόν, μετὰ ταῦτ' αἰδέσηται καὶ ἀφῇ, οὐκέτ' ἐκβαλεῖν κύριος τὸν αὐτόν ἐστιν. ' If anyone, having convicted a man of unintentional homicide and proved him unclean, afterwards pardons and releases him, he no longer has power to exile the same man.' (Almost the same words recur in D.38.22.)

The penalty imposed for *bouleusis* of homicide was the same as that for committing homicide with one's own hand. This is laid down by the law mentioned in And.1.94 (quoted on page 64) : ' a person who has planned is to be liable to the same treatment as one who has committed with his own hand'. Other passages (Ant.1.25, 27, Lys.13.56) also indicate that the penalty for *bouleusis* of intentional homicide was death. And the khoregos, accused of *bouleusis* of unintentional homicide, says that if he is condemned he will be required ' to keep away from Athens, holy places, games, and sacrifices ' (Ant.6.4 : εἴργεσθαι πόλεως, ἱερῶν, ἀγώνων, θυσιῶν), just like a person found to have committed unintentional homicide with his own hand ; more briefly, his accusers wish ' to drive me out of this land' (Ant.6.7 : ἐξελάσαι ἐκ τῆς γῆς ταύτης).

The penalty for killing a metic is stated by a late lexicographer to have been exile (*Dikon Onomata* in *Lex.Seg.*194.12-13). There is no other evidence to confirm or refute the statement.

It is nowhere stated what the penalty was for killing a foreigner. But occasionally we hear of a foreigner's being granted the privilege that, if anyone killed him, the killer was to suffer the same penalty as a killer of an Athenian citizen (e.g. *IG* ii² 32.9-14, 226.34-40, D.23.89), or that he was to be exiled from Athens and all other cities allied to Athens (e.g. *IG* ii² 24b.3-6, 73.6-12). This may imply that the normal penalty for killing a foreigner was less than for killing an Athenian citizen, and less than exile ; but not certainly so, since it may alternatively imply that normally the killer of a foreigner could be prosecuted in Athens only if the killing was committed in Athens, whereas the killer of an Athenian citizen could be prosecuted in Athens even when the killing was committed abroad (compare the rules about *androlepsion*, discussed on pages 27-31).

In *Against Neaira* it is stated that the aim of Stephanos in bringing a prosecution for the killing of a slave was ' to banish Apollodoros or disfranchise him ' (D.59.10 : ἐξελάσαι

Ἀπολλόδωρον ἢ ἀτιμῶσαι). Lykourgos says (65) that in early times the penalty for killing a slave was not merely a fine, and this seems to imply that the penalty might be merely a fine in the fourth century. So it is sufficiently clear that the offence of killing a slave had no one fixed penalty attached to it.

An unknown killer of course could not be punished at all. But there is some evidence that if any of the cities of the Athenian Empire in the second half of the fifth century was responsible for the killing of an Athenian citizen, that city had to pay a fine of five talents, even if the killer himself could not be identified. The chief piece of evidence is an inscription as restored by Adolf Wilhelm (*Attische Urkunden* iv 17-22).

SEG x 23.7-13.

ἐὰν δέ τις ἀπο[κτένει Ἀχελοῖον]-
[α ἒ τ]ὸν παῖδον τιν[ὰ ἐν τὸν πόλεόν πο]
[ὁπό]σον Ἀθεναῖο[ι κρατὸσιν, τὲν πόλ]-
[ιν π]έντε τάλαντ[α ὀφέλεν, ὁς ἐὰν Ἀθε]-
[ναῖ]ον τις ἀποθά[νει, καὶ τὰς τιμορί]-
[ας ἒ]ναι κατὰ τ[οὺτο καθάπερ Ἀθεναί]-
[ο ἀπο]θανόν[τος].

'If anyone kills Akheloion or any of his children anywhere in any of the cities which the Athenians rule, the city is to pay five talents, just as if an Athenian is killed, and the procedure for vengeance is to be the same as when an Athenian is killed.'

Wilhelm restored another inscription in a similar manner (*SEG* x 99). In Ar.*Peace* 164-72 Trygaios suggests that the state of Khios will have to pay five talents if he falls off his flying beetle and is killed, and this confirms that Wilhelm's restorations are on the right lines, even though some of the details are open to doubt. But the law remains obscure. It is not clear whether the state had to pay the fine only when an Athenian was killed inside its territory and the killer was unknown, or whether liability to the fine extended more widely than this. In the Aristophanes passage, Trygaios can see the man who may cause his death, who is in Peiraieus; so here the potential killer is not unknown, and Trygaios's death would not occur within the territory of Khios. Even that the potential killer is a Khian is not explicitly stated. But perhaps this passage is a comic exaggeration or distortion of the real legal situation. For example, there may have been some recent case in which Khios was compelled to pay five talents although there was really some doubt whether Khios had been responsible for an Athenian's death, and hence Aristophanes may here, for comic effect, be suggesting that Khios will have to pay five talents even for a death which has nothing to do with Khios at all; or other explanations of the joke are conceivable. We cannot be sure in what circumstances precisely a city became liable to a fine of five talents. (On this problem, see Russell Meiggs in *CR* lxiii [1949] 9-12, and G. E. M. de Ste Croix in *CQ* xi [1961] 268.) But at least it appears that in some circumstances a penalty for homicide might be exacted even when the killer was unknown.

A person who committed lawful homicide suffered no penalty. But when he had been acquitted, was he legally required to undergo religious purification? Plato ordains purification in cases of accidental killing in war and athletic contests (*Laws* 865b), but it is not safe to assume that Athenian law was the same as Plato's. The decree of Demophantos (And.1.96-8) lays down that a person who kills a traitor shall be 'pure and undefiled' (ὅσιος καὶ εὐαγής); and that this is intended to be a religious and not merely a legal ruling is shown by the words included in the oath, ' I shall consider him to be pure in the sight of both gods and spirits' (ὅσιον . . . καὶ πρὸς θεῶν καὶ δαιμόνων). The law of Eukrates has a similar expression (*SEG* xii 87.11 : ὅσιος). Lykourgos says that such a person was ' clean ', and Demosthenes says that according to Drakon's law anyone who committed homicide lawfully was ' clean ' (καθαρόν in Lyk. 125 and D.20.158 ; cf. D.9.44, 23.55). It is hard to see why anyone already pure should need to be purified. A number of scholars have taken the view that after lawful homicide, at any rate in some cases, religious purification was required (e.g. Philippi 62-3, Lipsius 618, Treston 153). The balance of evidence seems to me to favour the opposite view (which is taken by Hewitt, in *TAPA* xli 99-113, and Moulinier 84). But it is not conclusive, and it is possible that religious scruple sometimes caused purification to be performed even if the law declared it to be unnecessary.

XIII

APAGOGE AND GRAPHE

MY account of the five special homicide courts of the Areopagos, Palladion, Delphinion, Phreatto, and prytaneion, and
of the laws and legal procedure relating to them, is now complete. But there existed another way of bringing a killer
to justice, which did not involve these courts at all. Demosthenes, in his speech *Against Aristokrates*, after giving an
account of the five special homicide courts, goes on to describe a sixth method of legal action against a killer and
explain how Aristokrates's decree conflicts with it.

D.23.80 : εἰ πάντα ταῦτά τις ἠγνόηκεν, ἢ καὶ παρελη-
λύθασιν οἱ χρόνοι ἐν οἷς ἔδει τούτων ἕκαστα ποιεῖν, ἢ δι'
ἄλλο τι οὐχὶ βούλεται τούτους τοὺς τρόπους ἐπεξιέναι, τὸν
ἀνδροφόνον δ' ὁρᾷ περιιόντ' ἐν τοῖς ἱεροῖς καὶ κατὰ τὴν
ἀγοράν, ἀπάγειν ἔξεστιν εἰς τὸ δεσμωτήριον, οὐκ οἴκαδ'
οὐδ' ὅποι βούλεται, ὥσπερ σὺ δέδωκας. κἀνταῦθ' ἀπαχθεὶς
οὐδ' ὁτιοῦν, πρὶν ἂν κριθῇ, πείσεται, ἀλλ' ἐὰν μὲν ἁλῷ,
θανάτῳ ζημιωθήσεται, ἐὰν δὲ μὴ μεταλάβῃ τὸ πέμπτον
μέρος τῶν ψήφων ὁ ἀπαγαγών, χιλίας προσοφλήσει. 'If one
is ignorant of all these methods, or the various times for
employing them are past, or for any other reason one
does not wish to proceed in these ways, and one sees the
killer going around in the holy places and in the agora,
one is permitted to arrest him and take him to prison, but
not take him home or anywhere one likes, as you have
allowed. And then after being arrested he will suffer no
penalty at all until he is tried. If he is convicted, he will

be punished by death ; but if the man who arrested him does not get one-fifth of the votes, he will also incur a fine of a thousand drakhmai.'

The case of Agoratos was one in which this procedure was used. Lysias 13 is a speech written to be delivered for the prosecution in this case. Agoratos is alleged to have caused the death of Dionysodoros by denouncing him to the Thirty. Dionysios, the brother of Dionysodoros, has proceeded against him by *apagoge*. This word ἀπαγωγή is used both for an arrest and for the written accusation which was made at the same time, and some features of the procedure are revealed in a passage in which the speaker (speaking in support or on behalf of Dionysios) tries to answer in advance a legal objection which he expects Agoratos to make.

Lys.13.85-7. ἀκούω δ' αὐτὸν καὶ ⟨τούτῳ⟩ διισχυρίζεσθαι, ὅτι " ἐπ' αὐτοφώρῳ " τῇ ἀπαγωγῇ ἐπιγέγραπται, ὃ πάντων ἐγὼ οἶμαι εὐηθέστατον· ὡς εἰ μὲν τὸ ἐπ' αὐτοφώρῳ μὴ προσεγέγραπτο, ἔνοχος ⟨ἂν⟩ ὢν τῇ ἀπαγωγῇ· διότι δὲ τοῦτο προσγέγραπται, [ἔνοχος ὢν] ῥᾳστώνην τινὰ οἴεται αὐτῷ εἶναι. τοῦτο δὲ οὐδὲν ἄλλο ἔοικεν ἢ ὁμολογεῖν ἀποκτεῖναι, μὴ ἐπ' αὐτοφώρῳ δέ, καὶ περὶ τούτου διισχυρίζεσθαι, ὥσπερ, εἰ μὴ ἐπ' αὐτοφώρῳ μέν, ἀπέκτεινε δέ, τούτου ἕνεκα δέον αὐτὸν σῴζεσθαι. δοκοῦσι δ' ἔμοιγε οἱ ἔνδεκα οἱ παραδεξάμενοι τὴν ἀπαγωγὴν ταύτην, ⟨οὐκ⟩ οἰόμενοι 'Αγοράτῳ συμπράττειν καὶ τότε διισχυριζομένῳ, σφόδρα ὀρθῶς ποιῆσαι Διονύσιον τὴν ἀπαγωγὴν ἀπάγοντ' ἀναγκάζοντες προσγράψασθαι τό γε ἐπ' αὐτοφώρῳ· ἢ πῶς οὐκ ἂν εἴη ⟨ὃς⟩ πρῶτον μὲν ἐναντίον πεντακοσίων [ἐν τῇ βουλῇ], εἶτα πάλιν ἐναντίον 'Αθηναίων ἀπάντων [ἐν τῷ δήμῳ] ἀπογράψας τινὰς ἀποκτείνειε καὶ αἴτιος γένοιτο τοῦ θανάτου; . . . ὥστε πῶς οὐκ ἐπ' αὐτοφώρῳ σὺ εἶ ὁ ἀποκτείνας; 'I hear that he is basing an argument also on the ground that

leave little opportunity for any kind of homicide prosecution to be brought by a non-relative. Thus both *dikai* and
graphai arising from homicide were usually brought by the
relatives of the killed person. A more important way in
which the procedure by *apagoge* and *graphe* differed from a
dike for homicide was that it went to an ordinary heliastic
court instead of one of the special homicide courts. A
heliastic jury may often have been less successful than the
Areopagos or the ephetai in reaching a fair verdict.

As the account of Demosthenes shows, the charge brought
by this procedure was not merely one of killing, but of
behaving in a certain way after killing. In this respect it
closely resembled the procedure used against a man thought
guilty of submitting himself to homosexual acts (ἑταίρησις).
Such a man had a body that was not clean (καθαρόν). He
was forbidden to hold an arkhonship, a priesthood, or any
other public office, to make a proposal in the assembly, and
so forth. As long as he refrained from these activities, he
apparently suffered no penalty ; but if he did do any of the
forbidden things, he could be prosecuted by a *graphe* (γραφὴ
ἑταιρήσεως), and the penalty was death (Ais.1.19-20, 87,
D.22.30). Likewise with the killer. His hands were not
clean (μὴ καθαρὸς τὰς χεῖρας, or a similar expression, in
Ant.5.11, 82, And.1.95, D.24.60). He was forbidden to
enter the holy places or the agora, to touch holy water, and
so forth (D.20.158). As long as he avoided these things,
legal action against him could be taken only by the slow
procedure of the special homicide courts ; but otherwise he
could be prosecuted by a *graphe*, and the penalty was death
(D.23.80). Though the charge in such a *graphe* was not
killing alone, we might expect, if the analogy with ἑταίρησις holds, that it would be called simply γραφὴ φόνου.

This explains a passage of Polydeukes which has sometimes caused difficulty. Polyd.8.40, giving a catalogue of offences for which *graphai* might be brought, puts homicide (φόνου) first in the list. Some scholars have thought that all homicide cases were *dikai*, not *graphai*, and that Polydeukes is wrong or confused. But the evidence of D.23.80 shows that he is right, and that γραφαὶ φόνου did exist. On the other hand, I hesitate to use as evidence a passage in *Lexeis Rhetorikai* (*Lex.Seg.* 250.5-9) which runs : καὶ τοὺς ἀγομένους ἐπὶ κακουργήμασι παρελάμβανον [sc. οἱ ἕνδεκα] κλέπτας καὶ ἀνδραποδιστὰς καὶ φονεῖς· καὶ τοὺς μὲν ὁμολογοῦντας θανάτῳ ἐζημίουν, τοὺς δὲ ἀμφισβητοῦντας εἰσῆγον εἰς δικαστήριον. This seems to imply that arrested killers who admitted guilt might be executed without trial, which appears to be at variance with D.23.80. And later in the same lexicon (*Lex.Seg.*310.14-17) there is a slightly different account with no mention of killers : οἱ ἕνδεκα τοὺς κλέπτας καὶ τοὺς λωποδύτας καὶ ἀνδραποδιστὰς ὁμολογοῦντας μὲν ἀποκτιννύουσιν, ἀντιλέγοντας δὲ εἰσάγουσιν εἰς τὸ δικαστήριον. The earlier passage is evidently confused, and it would be unwise to draw from it any conclusion about homicide.

In our manuscripts of Lysias, the speech *Against Agoratos* is given the title Κατὰ ᾿Αγοράτου ἐνδείξεως. The procedure of *endeixis* was slightly different from that of *apagoge*. In *apagoge* the accuser himself arrested the accused and took him to the appropriate official. In *endeixis* the accuser merely reported the offence to the official, and the official made the arrest. But the effect of both was much the same, and from the legal point of view the difference is not very important. So it is quite possible that *endeixis* as well as *apagoge* was allowed against a killer found in the holy places or the agora. The title of Lysias's speech is very poor evidence, because it is most uncertain whether the titles were given to the speeches in Lysias's own time, and because this title is any-

K

way incorrect, since Lys.13.85-7 shows that Agoratos was prosecuted not by *endeixis* but by *apagoge*. But Polydeukes says that *endeixis* was used against killers (Polyd.8.50 : μάλιστα δὲ τοὺς ὀφείλοντας τῷ δημοσίῳ ἐνεδείκνυσαν, ἢ τοὺς κατιόντας ὅποι μὴ ἔξεστιν, ἢ τοὺς ἀνδροφόνους).

Some have thought that the procedure used against Agoratos was used also in the Herodes case. But this is incorrect. Antiphon 5 is a speech written to be delivered by the accused man. Part of it (Ant.5.8-19) is devoted to an argument that the accusers have employed the wrong legal procedure. They ought, the speaker says, to have brought a δίκη φόνου; instead they have prosecuted him by *endeixis* and *apagoge* (the words ἐνδεδειγμένος and ἀπαγωγή are both used in Ant.5.9) as a ' wrongdoer ' (κακοῦργος). He recounts a number of differences between this procedure and the one that ought to have been used. One of them is that he has been imprisoned until his trial, whereas persons accused of homicide in the normal way are free to go into exile to avoid trial if they wish. Another is that in the present trial the penalty, if he is convicted, will be fixed by the jury ; but in the kind of trial which ought to have been held the death penalty is fixed by law. (The words in Ant.5.10 are τίμησίν μοι ἐποίησαν, ἀνταποθανεῖν τοῦ νόμου κειμένου τὸν ἀποκτείναντα. This is not contradicted by the words ἀξιώσεις με ἀποκτεῖναι a little later, in Ant.5.16, since they mean ' you will ask the court to execute me ', and refer to the later stage of the trial, in which the penalty will be decided.) This is a decisive difference from the procedure described in D.23.80, for there Demosthenes states that the penalty in a γραφὴ φόνου is death, not that it varies at the discretion of the jury. So the procedure used in this case is not γραφὴ φόνου (or ἀπαγωγὴ φόνου); it is ἔνδειξις κακουργίας (or ἀπαγωγὴ κακουργίας) which, just as the speaker claims, is not a correct procedure when the alleged offence is homicide. (The argument of Glotz *La solidarité* 430, that the Eleven would not have allowed the arrest if the procedure followed had not been a proper one for homicide, is not cogent. The Eleven were not judges ; if the accusers said that the arrested man was a ' wrongdoer ', the arrest would have to be allowed, and it would be for the jury to decide whether the act committed by the accused was ' wrongdoing ' or not.) The reason why the accusers in this case did not bring the same kind of prosecution as was brought against Agoratos may have been that they thought they could not claim that the accused was a killer ' manifestly '. But the procedure used against ' wrongdoers ' deserves no place in an account of homicide law.

The case of Menestratos is one in which the *apagoge* procedure for homicide seems to have been used. Like Agoratos, Menestratos denounced a number of men to the Thirty. After the restoration of the democracy in 403 he was convicted as a killer and executed.

> Lys.13.56. ὑμεῖς δὲ πολλῷ χρόνῳ ὕστερον λαβόντες ἐν δικαστηρίῳ ὡς ἀνδροφόνον ὄντα, θάνατον δικαίως καταψηφισάμενοι τῷ δημίῳ παρέδοτε καὶ ἀπετυμπανίσθη. ' Much later you convicted him in a law-court as being a killer, and, justly condemning him to death, you handed him over to the executioner and he was put to death by the *tympanon.*'

Now, when the democracy was restored an amnesty was declared, in accordance with which no one could thereafter be convicted or punished for an offence committed before the arkhonship of Eukleides (403/2), with certain exceptions ; one of the exceptions was that a person who had committed homicide with his own hand was subject to trial and punishment in the normal way (*Ath.Pol.* 39.5-6 ; cf. And.1.87-94). Menestratos had not committed homicide with his own hand, and the deaths for which he was blamed occurred before 403/2. How then could he be condemned ' as being a killer ' ? He must have been accused, by the process of *apagoge* and *graphe*, of frequenting the holy places and the agora although manifestly a killer. The alleged killing had admittedly taken place before 403/2 ; but the offence of frequenting the holy places and the agora took place in or after 403/2, and so it could be argued that this offence was not subject to the amnesty. He was an Athenian citizen, of the deme Amphitrope (Lys.13.55), which refutes the theory (put forward by Glotz *La solidarité* 431-2) that this procedure could be used only against non-citizens.

In 411 Thrasyboulos and Apollodoros killed Phrynikhos, a leading member of the Four Hundred. Lykourgos describes what happened to them.

Lyk.112-13. Φρυνίχου γὰρ ἀποσφαγέντος νύκτωρ παρὰ τὴν κρήνην τὴν ἐν τοῖς οἰσύοις ὑπὸ 'Απολλοδώρου καὶ Θρασυβούλου, καὶ τούτων ληφθέντων καὶ εἰς τὸ δεσμωτήριον ἀποτεθέντων ὑπὸ τῶν τοῦ Φρυνίχου φίλων, αἰσθόμενος ὁ δῆμος τὸ γεγονὸς τούς τε εἰρχθέντας ἐξήγαγε, καὶ βασάνων γενομένων ἀνέκρινε καὶ ζητῶν τὸ πρᾶγμα εὗρε τὸν μὲν Φρύνιχον προδιδόντα τὴν πόλιν, τοὺς δ' ἀποκτείναντας αὐτὸν ἀδίκως εἰρχθέντας· καὶ ψηφίζεται ὁ δῆμος Κριτίου εἰπόντος . . . ' Phrynikhos was killed at night near the spring in the basket-market by Apollodoros and Thrasyboulos, and they were caught and put in the prison by Phrynikhos's family. When the people saw what had happened they brought them out of prison, and after questioning had taken place they held an inquiry, investigated the affair, and found that Phrynikhos was a traitor to the state, and his killers had been unjustly imprisoned.

On the proposal of Kritias the people decreed . . . ' [An account follows of a decree condemning Phrynikhos.]

Phrynikhos was killed in the summer of 411. But Thrasyboulos and Apollodoros were not imprisoned then. We know from other sources (Th.8.92.2, Lys.13.71) that on that occasion the killers escaped, and it was not even known who they were. Besides, the imprisonment and inquiry described by Lykourgos clearly belong to a time when the *demos* was in control, after the restoration of the democracy in 410. A more exact date can be obtained from epigraphical evidence. *IG* i² 110 is a decree conferring honours on Thrasyboulos and others associated with him in the killing of Phrynikhos ; it is dated by its prescript to the spring of 409. The decree which condemned Phrynikhos must belong to the same time. The likely explanation is that after the restoration of the democracy in 410 Thrasyboulos and Apollodoros returned to Athens and boasted of being the killers of Phrynikhos. The relatives of Phrynikhos tried to proceed against them by *apagoge*, alleging that they frequented the holy places and the agora although they were manifestly killers, but before the case could come to trial the people intervened and passed decrees declaring Phrynikhos to be a traitor and honouring those who killed him.

I conclude this chapter by summarizing the various ways in which *apagoge* might be used in connexion with homicide, drawing attention particularly to the features which distinguish them from one another.

A : If a proclamation had been made by the basileus ordering a man ' to keep away from the legal things ', and he was then (between the proclamation and the trial at one of the special homicide courts) found in the agora or any of the other places where he was forbidden to go, he might suffer *apagoge*.   He was tried, and if he was found guilty the penalty was fixed at the discretion of the court.   (D.24.105 ; see pages 26-7.)

B : If a man was ' manifestly ' a killer, and was found in the agora or other places where killers were forbidden to go, he might suffer *apagoge*, even if no proclamation or other legal action had previously been taken against him.   He was tried, and if he was found guilty the penalty was death.   An important difference between this kind of case and *A* is that in *B* it would be necessary for the accuser at the trial to prove that the accused was a killer, whereas in *A* it was presumably necessary only to prove that a proclamation had been made against him.   (Lys.13, D.23.80 ; see pages 130-9.)

C : If a man had been found guilty at a homicide trial and had gone (or ought to have gone) into exile, and then was found anywhere in Attica, he might suffer *apagoge* and be executed without trial by the thesmothetai.   (*IG* i² 115.30-1, D.23.28-31 ; see pages 121-2.)

A fourth kind of *apagoge*, by which a man was charged as a ' wrongdoer ' (κακοῦργος), was used against the man accused of killing Herodes ; but he argues, probably rightly, that this procedure was not proper in a case of homicide. (Ant.5.8-19 ; see pages 136-7.)

XIV

VENGEANCE, CLEANSING, AND DETERRENCE

It is not possible to dissect the whole body of Athenian homicide law and arrange the members in three neat piles labelled ' vengeance ', ' cleansing ', and ' deterrence '. This is because a good many of the law's provisions appear to serve two or even all three of these purposes, and we then have no way of telling which purpose or purposes were in the minds of the men who introduced them.

The death penalty is an outstanding example. When a killer is executed, this may be thought to be vengeance for the man he killed ; it may be thought to free the state from the pollution of the killer's presence ; and it may be thought to deter other prospective killers. We know that all three ideas were current in Athens, but we cannot know which was uppermost in the minds of the legislators who introduced or retained the death penalty. We have no ground for attributing the death penalty to any one of the three ideas to the exclusion of the others ; we have likewise no ground for saying that it was due to all three equally.

The same applies to the penalty of exile. If an unintentional killer is exiled, it may be thought that the person he killed is avenged, because the killer is suffering for his act. It may also be thought that the state is freed from pollution, because the killer no longer defiles it by his presence. And it may be thought that others who might in the future cause death by negligence will be induced to exercise greater care,

for fear of being exiled.   So the fact that the law imposed
exile does not tell us which motive, or motives, inspired the
law.   When a man was sentenced to exile, naturally the
sentence had to be enforced, and this explains the procedure
said to have been followed at the court in Phreatto ; the
exiled killer pleaded from a boat and was forbidden to land,
because if the exile already imposed on him were relaxed its
effect might be lessened, but that still does not tell us whether
the effect chiefly desired when exile was imposed was vengeance, cleansing, or deterrence.

Some modern writers have assumed that the only possible
reason for exiling a man is a desire to free the state from
pollution.   This assumption is false.   For example, Adkins
112 note 22, referring to the law ordaining exile for unintentional homicide (*IG* i² 115), writes : ' The extant portions
of the law of Draco do not in fact mention " pollution ",
but its existence is clearly implied '.   Actually the law contains no such clear implication ; it only contains regulations
about the prosecution and exile of killers.   Treston 247
writes : ' The court at Phreatto was clearly and unmistak-
ably derived from the religion of " pollution " '.   On the
contrary, the origin of the court is not at all clear, and it may
well be Treston himself who has made the mistake.   A
parallel from another country and another age may help to
illustrate the point.

Shakespeare *King Richard the Second* I iii 125-43.
   ' For that our kingdom's earth should not be soil'd
   With that dear blood which it hath fostered ;
   And for our eyes do hate the dire aspect
   Of civil wounds plough'd up with neighbours'
      sword ; . . .
   Therefore we banish you our territories :
   You, cousin Hereford, upon pain of life,

Till twice five summers have enrich'd our fields,
Shall not regreet our fair dominions,
But tread the stranger paths of banishment.'

Shakespeare actually gives Richard the words ' that our kingdom's earth should not be soil'd with that dear blood '. (The Athenian law about unintentional homicide contains no statement of purpose as explicit as this one.) If these words had been written by an Athenian, it would be very easy to take them as a reference to religious pollution. But who will maintain, on the basis of these words, that a doctrine of religious pollution was fundamental to English homicide law of the Plantagenet or of the Shakespearean period ? It is perfectly plain that the purpose Richard states for imposing exile on Bolingbroke and Norfolk is simply the avoidance of future killing. So in Athens too we must at least recognize the possibility that fear of pollution was not the reason for imposing exile.

What about lawful killing ? In certain circumstances a man who killed a traitor, a paramour of a female relative, a nocturnal thief, an opponent in an athletic contest, and so on, had committed homicide lawfully and went unpunished. In these cases the person killed did not deserve vengeance, because he had himself committed an offence. (If it seems unplausible to say that a man killed in an athletic contest deserved no vengeance, look at D.23.54 : ' If the man was too weak to stand the struggle to win, the legislator thought that what happened to him was his own fault, and so did not allow him to be avenged.') At the same time, no pollution had been incurred. (Compare the oath prescribed by the decree of Demophantos in And.1.97 : ' I shall consider him to be pure in the sight of both gods and spirits . . . ') And there was no need for such killers to be deterred. So who can say which was the chief motive behind the rules about lawful homicide ? A stone or a falling branch that killed a man could not be deterred by law ; but when the phylobasileis cast it beyond the frontier of Attica, were they performing ritual vengeance for the dead man, or were they freeing the country from a polluted object ?

When a man was killed, his family was required to take legal action. This may have been to ensure that the dead man was avenged, or to ensure that the state was freed from pollution, or to discourage prospective killers from thinking that they might escape punishment. Until his trial the accused killer had to avoid the agora, the holy places, holy water, and so on. Perhaps this was because his presence would pollute those places. But Demosthenes thought otherwise.

D.20.157-8. φέρε γὰρ πρὸς Διός, τί μάλιστ᾽ ἂν ἀπευξαί-μεθα πάντες, καὶ τί μάλιστ᾽ ἐν ἅπασι διεσπούδασται τοῖς νόμοις; ὅπως μὴ γενήσονται οἱ περὶ ἀλλήλους φόνοι, περὶ ὧν ἐξαίρετος ἡ βουλὴ φύλαξ ἡ ἐν Ἀρείῳ πάγῳ τέτακται. ἐν τοίνυν τοῖς περὶ τούτων νόμοις ὁ Δράκων φοβερὸν κατα-σκευάζων καὶ δεινὸν τό τιν᾽ αὐτόχειρ᾽ ἄλλον ἄλλου γίγνεσθαι, καὶ γράφων χέρνιβος εἴργεσθαι τὸν ἀνδροφόνον, σπονδῶν, κρατήρων, ἱερῶν, ἀγορᾶς, πάντα τἄλλα διελθὼν οἷς μάλιστ᾽ ἄν τινας ᾤετ᾽ ἐπισχεῖν τοῦ τοιοῦτόν τι ποιεῖν . . . 'Well, I ask you, what should we all most earnestly pray against, and in all the laws what end is the most eagerly sought ? That people may not kill one another. Of this the council on the Areopagos has special charge. So in his laws about this Drakon, making it a terrible and fearful thing for one person to kill another with his own hand, and ordain-ing that the killer should keep away from holy water, libations, bowls of wine, holy places, and the agora, and listing everything else which he thought would best restrain people from that kind of offence . . .'

Clearly Demosthenes thinks that the purpose of excluding killers from those places is not the protection of the places and other people from pollution but the deterrence of future killers. He may be wrong. The legislator, whether Drakon or not, lived long before Demosthenes, and Demosthenes may be mistaken about his intentions. But we have no better evidence than Demosthenes had for guessing what his intentions were. Still less can we claim to have better evidence than Demosthenes had about why the rule was retained in the fourth century. Modern writers have commonly assumed that the motive for excluding killers from the agora and other places can only have been fear of pollution. But the words of Demosthenes show that this should not be taken for granted.

The basileus, whose other duties were mostly religious, had charge of homicide trials, and they were always held in a holy place and in the open air (*Ath.Pol.* 57.4 : ἐν ἱερῷ καὶ ὑπαίθριοι). This may mean that homicide was regarded as a religious offence. But appeasing spirits of vengeance and cleansing from pollution are both religious acts, and so the religious trappings of homicide trials do not tell us which of these two ideas prevailed when the procedure was laid down. Weinreich (in *Hermes* lvi 326-31) suggests that trials were held in the open air in order that those present might be purified by the sun and rain. But this is not the only possible reason. According to Antiphon, the purpose of holding the trial in the open air was that the jury and prosecutor might not share a roof (ὁμωρόφιος γίγνηται) with the killer (Ant.5.11). Becoming ὁμωρόφιος, or sharing a roof, was a symbol of friendship (cf. Ant.6.39-40, quoted on page 31, D.22.2, quoted on pages 9-10, and D.18.287); to refuse to share a roof with a killer may have meant only that the killer was an enemy, from whom vengeance was to be exacted. So here again either vengeance or cleansing may be the dominant motive. Other aspects of trial procedure may have been due primarily to a desire to ensure that the verdict reached was the right one. For example, the *prodikasiai* at which cases were repeatedly investigated before trial, the special juries of the Areopagos and the ephetai, the special oaths demanded of the parties and the witnesses to discourage lying, and the rules about the relevance of speeches—all these helped a just decision to be made, but they tell us nothing about whether the purpose of making the decision was vengeance, cleansing, or deterrence.

The use of *apagoge* and *graphe* as an alternative to prosecution in the special homicide courts may possibly have been instituted later than the other procedure. What was its purpose? It could be used against a person who was found in the agora or the holy places (D.23.80) when 'manifestly' a killer (Lys.13.85-7). The most significant difference between prosecuting a person by this method and by the other seems to have been that this method was quicker and less complicated. Demosthenes introduces his account of it with the words : 'If one is ignorant of all these methods, or the various times for employing them are past, or for any other reason one does not wish to proceed in these ways . . .' (D.23.80). Prosecution in the special homicide courts involved the long and slow process of proclamations and *prodikasiai*. It could give rise to tiresome delays, as the prosecutors of the khoregos found (Ant.6.38, 42), and it was so complex that the trierarkhos did not fully understand it until he had consulted the exegetai and the inscribed 'laws of Drakon' (D.47.68-71). The object of introducing the use of *apagoge* and *graphe* may have been simply an increase of speed and efficiency in cases in which the more complicated process was unnecessary (because the accused was

' manifestly ' a killer). If so, this too tells us nothing about the purpose of condemning a killer.

Thus a large part of Athenian homicide law is discouragingly unrevealing about the motives which inspired it. But there remain a few less ambiguous pointers.

In the first place, it is clear that the persons who framed the laws (or some of them) thought it right to take into account the intention of the killer. One of the most fundamental distinctions in the whole system is that between intentional and unintentional homicide. This distinction has nothing to do with vengeance for the dead man, and it has nothing to do with cleansing from pollution. If an innocent man is killed, it makes no difference to him whether the killer meant to kill him or not ; in either case he is dead, and he did not deserve to die, and if he deserves vengeance in the one case he deserves it equally in the other. Pollution is caused by the act of killing, whether it is intended or not. The fictional case in the *Second Tetralogy* is one of unintentional homicide ; yet the prosecutor still claims that both vengeance and cleansing are required, and asks the jury ' to pity the untimely end of the dead boy, and not to let the whole city remain polluted by this man ' (Ant.3a.2). Why then was a more lenient penalty imposed for unintentional than for intentional homicide ? And why was no penalty at all imposed on a man who killed a fellow-citizen by mistake for an enemy in war, or on a doctor in whose hands a patient died ? Because the penalty was adjusted according to the intention of the killer. And when the consideration is not the deserts of the dead man or the religious condition of the state but the intention of the killer, we are no longer in the sphere of vengeance or of cleansing but in the sphere of deterrence. So there is no doubt that deterrence was not merely an aim which orators claimed to be desirable but one which was fundamentally embodied in the law.

If a killed man before he died absolved his killer, no prosecution for homicide could follow (D.37.59). This rule is plainly based on the belief that the purpose of punishment was to provide vengeance for the killed man, and that if the killed man did not desire vengeance there was no need to punish the killer. There is perhaps no other part of the whole body of Athenian homicide law which could not, with some ingenuity, be attributed to desire for cleansing or for deterrence, to support an argument that vengeance played no part in the law. But this rule about absolution by the killed person refutes such an argument, and proves beyond question that vengeance required by the killed person was one of the principles on which the law was founded.

What about cleansing from pollution ? Demosthenes says that when an unintentional killer was pardoned and allowed to return from exile, the law ordained ' sacrifice, cleansing, and certain other actions ' (D.23.72). This proves that the doctrine of pollution was recognized in the law. The surprising thing, however, at least to those familiar with the modern literature on this subject, is that this passage is, as far as I can discover, the only one which proves it. There are some other provisions in the law which may have been inspired by a belief in pollution, but not a single other which must. All others could be explained on the assumption that vengeance and deterrence were the only two aims of the legislators, and that pollution was a matter with which the law, as distinct from priests, philosophers, poets, orators, and private persons, was not concerned.

Furthermore, there are two ways in which the law seems positively to ignore pollution. When the khoregos was first accused of causing the death of Diodotos, the basileus refused to accept the charge because his year of office had less than three months to run ; and until the charge was made again to the basileus of the following year the khoregos suffered no legal disability, but was able to proceed with his prosecution of Philinos and others (Ant.6.38). This delay had nothing to do with the guilt or innocence of the khoregos or with the ulterior motives of Philokrates in accusing him ; the rule must have applied equally to anyone accused of homicide. It appears that pollution was no obstacle to legal activity. If the khoregos was guilty of causing the death of Diodotos, he was polluted during the last three months of the year as much as at any other time. But the law did not care.

When an Athenian was killed outside Attica, steps were taken, in the shape of *androlepsiai*, to get the killer extradited to Athens for trial (D.23.82, Polyd.8.50-1, *Lexeis Rhetorikai* in *Lex.Seg.*213.30-214.2). A killer polluted the state by his presence, not by his absence. If the legislator was concerned with pollution, one would expect to find that the killer was forbidden to enter Attica. In fact the law demanded that he should enter Attica. This is a second kind of case in which the law took no account of pollution.

If it is the case that one part of Athenian homicide legislation assumes that a killer is polluted, whereas other parts assume that he is not polluted, this means that it contains an inherent contradiction. It is very unlikely that a body of law containing this kind of internal contradiction was all due to one man (whether Drakon or anyone else), and rather unlikely that it all originated at one time. Almost nothing can be known about Athenian homicide law before the age of the orators ; but, to judge from these contradictory elements, there does appear to be a strong probability that part of it originated before the period when the idea of pollution became current in Athens, and part afterwards. At what date the idea of pollution reached Athens it is impossible to say. There are several provisions in the law which may have been first introduced after the idea became current, but, as I have said, only one which must : the rule that a killer returning from exile should undergo a ritual of purification. This ritual is, in a sense, distinct from the rest of the legal procedure. (It is noteworthy that Aiskhylos keeps it quite separate in the *Eumenides* : Orestes is purified at Delphoi at the beginning of the play, but his legal trial takes place in Athens a considerable time afterwards.) It is therefore quite conceivable that all the rest of the legislation on homicide was in being before the idea of pollution appeared in Athens, and that the requirement of a ceremony of cleansing was the only later addition. Thus it is unwise to take for granted that a belief in pollution was fundamental to Athenian homicide law. It is possible that it was no more than the subject of an appendix.

INDEX OF PASSAGES

INDEX OF GREEK WORDS

INDEX OF SUBJECTS